MW00675592

RIGHT OFF
THE BAT

An intimate and humorous look
into the world of sporting goods
marketing

JIM DARBY

ISBN: 978-0-9848352-6-3

Published by Margin Dot Press
www.margindotpress.com

Manufactured in the United States of America

Table of Contents

FOREWORD

One day while visiting my wife and me, Jim Darby said, "Skip, when I'm sitting on airplanes (and he does that very often) I have written down so many stories and experiences that I hope to write a book one day." A lot of people say that but never get around to it. Jim is not like that—I knew he would do it.

So my good friend Jim Darby has written a book. Knowing "Darbs" for over 30 years, I was certain the book would be a great read. I knew it would include many wonderful stories of great athletes and the role that he played with each of them. I was also certain the book would be comprised of some of the same qualities he employed as a player, coach, and high level administrator promoting products for Easton Sports.

When I first met Jim, something just clicked, and I found that he knows what he is talking about when it comes to athletics. More than that, Jim has always been able to share his wisdom. He has a gift of sharing his philosophy simply, directly, and in a manner accessible to everyone. That's why this book is so much fun.

He can be intense when necessary, but always pleasant. He would never allow mediocrity and definitely seeks excellence in all he does. He is about focus, belief, and vision. Jim has defended non-wood ball bats against ridiculous accusations and, with his penchant for facts and finding the truth, has won out every time.

Like most of those who are successful, Jim understands people. What a joy it is to be around Jim, whether you are one of the great ones like Wayne Gretzky, John Elway, Pete Rose, Joe Montana, or just an assistant coach of a high school or college baseball team. He is always the same person—bright, funny, compassionate, and consumed with the love of sports and his family. Not many people that I have met over a 50-year athletic career have had the personality and charisma of Jim Darby. You will find that here within these pages.

In over 40 years as a player, coach, and administrator, Jim Darby's dignity has never diminished. His integrity always remained intact, and, above all, he has always been honest. Along with so many other coaches and athletes that have dealt with Darbs, we have always been great friends. No one in sports has more friends than Jim Darby.

Funny stories? Jim has many—his times with Rickey Henderson, Goose Gossage, Will Clark, and others are hilarious. I found this book to be very funny, informative, insightful, and a quick read. You will laugh at how Jim got into the business. Throughout the entire book, Jim is always himself. He is never afraid to admit a failure and second-guess himself on how he could have done a better job.

Jim Darby has gained respect with a very simple method—by his personal example. He's worked harder and has been more dedicated, loyal, concerned, meticulous, and enthusiastic than most of the other people I have ever worked with.

In the end, Jim is simply a winner. If I were back coaching a baseball team, I would have no problem putting him in the game to pitch with a one-run lead in the bottom of the ninth. He's the guy you want to take the last shot in a tie basketball game, or the guy you would give the ball to when your team is a yard from the goal line and it's the last play of the game. In short, like his book, Jim Darby always comes through.

Skip Bertman

Skip Bertman won five NCAA championships while serving as the baseball coach at LSU. A member of the American Baseball Coaches Association Hall of Fame, he also served as the head coach of the United States Olympic team at the 1996 games in Atlanta.

CHAPTER ONE

The *Sports Illustrated* Effect

Sporting goods promotion people all play the same game. Our job is to create demand for the brand—the more exposure the logo gets, the more consumers want it.

Today that visibility is mainly achieved through television exposure. With the explosion of cable channels, hardly a day goes by when fans cannot see a football, baseball, basketball, or hockey game. ESPN even has a channel devoted to many of the great games played in the past.

This was not the case in the 1980s and early 1990s. People in my profession lived for the pictures in newspapers and sports magazines because they gave validity to our existence and could be measured in terms of dollars. Taking out an ad in a major metropolitan newspaper costs companies thousands of dollars, so when a baseball player was pictured holding a Mizuno ball glove, a football player in the shoes, or a hockey player scoring with an Easton stick, that was gold. Free gold. Needless to say, we went to great extremes to make those pictures happen.

One Saturday evening in November 1986, I was at home in Oakland, California, trying to plug a leak in my roof when the phone rang. On the line was Roger Craig, the 49ers' All-Pro running back.

"Jimbo, I screwed up, man!" he exclaimed, his voice full of panic. "I forgot to pack my turf shoes. You gotta get me some shoes!"

Delivering shoes was simple enough—except that Roger was calling from New Orleans, where the Niners were preparing to play the Saints the next day. Craig was one of the most photographed players in the NFL, and every game was an opportunity for brand exposure. Remembering there was a pair of size 11 generic turf shoes in my sample locker, I hopped into my car and drove the thirty-five miles to our Burlingame office. The shoes were generic in the sense that they were white with a white logo; for any good exposure, I would have to paint the Mizuno logo in the 49er red.

As I was finishing my best Leonardo DiVinci on the shoes, Doug Kelly, president of the company, happened to walk in, planning to catch up on paper work. I told him why he had caught me red-handed (quite literally!), and the next thing I knew, the president and senior vice president of a major team supplier were driving to the airport with football shoes hanging out the windows of the car so the paint would dry. Now that's what I call executive power!

We made it just in time for the shoes to board Delta's last flight to New Orleans, due to arrive just before dawn. Our Louisiana sales rep was thrilled when I called to notify him that he had to pick up the shoes at the Delta counter at 6:00 a.m. and then deliver them to the Niners' downtown hotel. What else could he have possibly wanted to do on a Sunday morning?

When Craig went down to the team breakfast the next morning, the shoes were waiting for him. And later that afternoon, in front of a large regional television audience, he scored the winning touchdown.

So was it worth all the fuss to get the shoes to Craig? The next day, the *San Francisco Chronicle* ran a half-page color photo of Craig crossing the goal line with one foot up in the air and the Mizuno logo clear as day. Damn right it was worth it.

While the newspapers were a great vehicle for brand exposure, *Sports Illustrated* was the bible. An ad in *SI* was worth tens of thousands of dollars, and a shot on the cover was, as the saying goes, priceless.

We hit our first big jackpot in April of 1981 when *Sports Illustrated* ran a feature on the upstart Oakland Athletics. The cover featured the five starting pitchers, and three of them, Matt Keough, Rick Langford, and Mike Norris, all had the Mizuno ball gloves prominently displayed; in addition, Keough and Langford had on the Mizuno cleats. I went to every newsstand I could find and bought over 200 copies of the magazine, which were immediately sent out to our sales reps and top retail customers nationwide.

The story didn't end there, though. Four years later, on a Saturday in 1985, I received a call from Matt Keough, who told me *Sports Illustrated* was planning another piece on the A's five aces. This time, however, it would be a story on what had gone wrong. Each of them had struggled after the 1981 season. Most experts put the blame on former manager Billy Martin for over-throwing his starters. *SI*'s plan was to pose them in the exact same position as on the 1981 cover, and Keough called to make sure the products would be the same, which meant that Mizuno received double-bang for the buck from the Oakland A's five aces.

A different *Sports Illustrated* cover shot actually put me in hot water, courtesy of the paranoia of the National Football League. The NFL is extremely protective about what is seen on the field, and they want all the players to look the same.

Right around 1992, Doug Kelly, our president, negotiated a licensing deal giving Easton the rights to be the official wristband of the NFL "Quarterbacks Club." The sales of wristbands do not generate huge revenues, but they can certainly generate tremendous brand exposure. Just about every picture in the newspapers and magazines showed the hands of players, and—if turned the right way—the company logo just popped right out at the reader. Case in point, the year-end issue of *Sports Illustrated* in 1990 featured Joe Montana as "Athlete of the Year," and there were five photos of the Niners' star quarterback vividly displaying the "Diamond E" logo. I don't think these shots sold a whole lot of wristbands, but I guarantee it put the Easton brand in people's minds—particularly the sporting goods retail buyers.

There was one small problem. The deal Kelly negotiated allowed us to put the logos on only one side of the wristband, and the QB Club logo had to be prominent, which meant that the Easton logo would be so small that visibility for the company would be negligible at best.

As previously mentioned, the NFL was really uptight about uniformity. The League actually had people assigned to patrol the sidelines, and players in non-approved products received fines. Companies that distributed products that did not conform to the NFL guidelines then received nasty letters or got a phone call from Gene Goldberg, the man in charge of licensing. Gene was a good guy but had a job to do, and no one wanted to get a call from Gene.

Throughout the 1994 regular season, Steve Young, the 49ers' quarterback, wore the regular "Diamond E" wristbands—the bands that did not have the QB Club logo that our license called for—yet I never received a call from Gene Goldberg for one simple reason: Young wore his wristbands with the Easton logo on the inside, not the outside. The logo was never visible.

Of course, that was not what I wanted to see. It didn't do me any good to see a blank on the outside of Young's wrists. One day at the Niners' practice, I asked Steve why he wore the bands in that manner.

"It's simple," he explained. "What's a wristband for? To wipe sweat off my forehead. And if the logo is on the outside of the band, it scratches my head."

It made sense, but even if it didn't, I couldn't have told him he was wrong.

Young continued, "Quit complaining. You'll get your exposure." And with that, he sauntered off to the training room.

The Niners ended up capturing the NFC championship a few weeks later and headed to Miami to play the San Diego Chargers in the Super Bowl. The Super Bowl is the single most-watched event in the United States and is the pride of the NFL. The League wants everything to be perfect, including what shows up on the players. It came as no surprise when I received a call during the week prior to the game from Gene Goldberg. "You know the rules, so I don't want to see any unauthorized wristbands on the field. I mean none," he emphasized.

I got the message and made it very clear to our promo team that only QB Club wristbands were to be distributed to the players of the 49ers and Chargers. Certainly, I wanted to see the "Diamond E" logo on the field, but I also didn't want my rear end handed to me by Goldberg.

On Super Bowl Sunday, the Niners absolutely crushed the Chargers, and Young was named the Most Valuable Player. All the pictures in the newspapers the next day showed players wearing the QB Club logo bands, and every shot of Young was just like those of the regular season—nothing but white, as the logo was on the inside part of his wrist.

Four days later, the Atlanta Super Show, the largest trade show in the sporting goods industry, opened up. I was checking into the Peachtree Plaza Hotel when Sandy Sandoval, one of our promo managers, came rushing up to me, waving the new issue of *Sports Illustrated*. He was really fired up because on the cover, perfectly positioned with his arms raised in triumph, was Steve Young, and right in the middle of the page—bright as day—were the two Easton "Diamond E" logos on his wristbands. Young was right—we got our exposure. But all I could think at that moment was, "I'm dead."

I prayed that Gene Goldberg would not be at the show. But, alas, he was, and he had a scowl on his face when I spotted him coming down the aisle toward our booth. I had to do some serious tap dancing to get around that one.

The controversy (and my resulting panic) didn't keep us from scouring downtown Atlanta to buy every copy of the magazine we could get our hands on. Our top retail customers went home with a copy of that *Sports Illustrated* issue—I guarantee it!

Steve Young was right—we got our exposure. Big time!

CHAPTER
TWO

How in the World Did I Get Into This?

In the early 70s, when I was trying to hang on as a ballplayer at the University of California, there was a man by the name of Tom Christiansen, who served as a representative for the Rawlings Sporting Goods Company. Occasionally, he came by the field to show his wares and shoot the breeze with the coaches. Realizing that I barely had a shot making the Cal team, much less ever having a chance to play pro baseball, I thought Christiansen had the coolest job in the world.

Little did I know.

I was born in Los Angeles but spent most of my childhood in Moraga, California, a small town located approximately thirty miles east of San Francisco. Like many boys growing up in the early 60s, sports were a major part of my daily existence—at least the three major sports (football, basketball, and baseball). When one season ended, I jumped to the next. During summers, my friends and I hopped on our bikes at nine in the morning and headed straight to the nearest ball field, where we made up every conceivable baseball game we could imagine. We played until it was time to go home and eat an early dinner, changed into our youth team uniforms, and then headed back to the ballpark. There was no such thing as travel teams or elite teams. Kids played to, well, just play—and to emulate sports heroes, which, in my case, meant Willie Mays and Juan Marichal of the San Francisco Giants and Sandy Koufax of the Los Angeles Dodgers.

I would like to say that I was an accomplished high school athlete, but, unfortunately, that wasn't quite the case. I managed to earn letters in three sports: cross-country, basketball, and baseball—all without fanfare. The highlight play of my high school career was the time I led our varsity basketball team out onto the floor for the second-half warm-ups following an inspirational speech by our coach. I hadn't even left the bench in the first half, so I thought I should show the coach and all the fans how I could dazzle them with a warm-up lay up. I dribbled the ball to the hoop, jumped as high as I could, and let the ball roll off my fingertips into the basket. It was poetry in air. There was only one problem: The man sweeping the floor hadn't quite finished and was standing directly under the rim. My feet came down on top of his broom, which was at a 45-degree angle to the floor. SNAP! Both the sweeper and I went crashing to the floor, and the broom ended up in about five pieces. It was a hell of a play if I say so myself.

Although my dream had always been to attend the University of California, Berkeley, my high school grades dictated another course. Somehow, baseball coach Larry Potter of California Western University got my name and offered me a partial scholarship. So off to San Diego I went.

As a freshman, I didn't get a whole lot of playing time on the varsity team. There was one game on the schedule, though, that Coach Potter didn't want to use up his experienced pitchers, which was the game against the Marine Corps team at the training center in San Diego. The game didn't count in the regular standings, so the philosophy was to throw the sacrificial lamb out there to see what he could do. That meant me.

One important thing to know about the Marine baseball team in 1970 is that it was damn good. And mostly made up of minor leaguers who weren't able to avoid the draft and so used the team as their way of staying out of Vietnam. They liked nothing better than beating up on snot-nosed, long-haired college boys.

When I took the mound for the bottom of the first inning, I looked out beyond the center field fence and saw men training with pongee sticks. They were beating the hell out of each other. I remember thinking to myself, "Stay in college, stay in college…"

Unbelievably, by the seventh inning, we were leading 6-1. Coach Potter figured he couldn't play his luck too far, so he yanked me out of there and inserted a senior by the name of Scott Lee to finish the job.

Lee did more than just that. He came up to bat in the top of the eighth (there was no designated hitter in those days); when the pitch was thrown, he shut his eyes, swung from his ass, and connected, blasting a two-run homer far over the left field fence. We all hooted and hollered while Scottie laughed and pumped his fist as he rounded the bases.

That was the wrong thing to do when playing the Marines.

Our next batter, our lead-off man Phil Vetter, had just come back from a serious eye injury that he had suffered from a bad-hop grounder. We all should have known what was coming, but we were just a bunch of innocent college kids who were having fun cheering on our winning team. The pitcher wound up and threw the first pitch. Even from the dugout, I heard the thud of the impact as the ball slammed into Phil's helmet. It was an ugly scene and put an end to a very good (not to mention young) shortstop's career. That pitch taught me a valuable lesson: I would never take the game for granted again.

My dream to attend Cal came true about a year later when, through the efforts of Assistant Coach Del Youngblood, I was able to transfer from Cal Western. Unfortunately, my playing time at Cal was cut short for two reasons: First, the NCAA transfer rules dictated that I had to sit out for a year and a half, which was a major bummer; second—and more truthful—is that when I did get the chance to pitch, I was flat-out horrible. I was so damned nervous when I finally got in that I couldn't throw a strike if my life depended on it.

I had one good experience on the field, though. In the early 70s, it was tradition that the Cal Bears played an exhibition game against the Oakland Athletics every spring. On April 17, 1972, the game was all set to be played at Cal's Evans Diamond until the Teamsters staged a strike on the Berkeley campus, which meant the game had to be moved to the Oakland Coliseum. The move certainly wasn't good for student attendance, but the players loved it because we were going to play in a major league stadium.

Each Cal pitcher got to throw one inning against the A's, and my turn came in the seventh inning (which goes to show my ranking in the pecking order). It was a successful inning, though, with no runs, no hits, and one walk. It was the most exciting experience of my baseball career; 40-plus years later, I can still remember the four players I faced: Brant Alyea, Bobby Brooks, Mike Hegan, and Larry Brown. They weren't exactly the murderers' row of A's stars (like Reggie Jackson, Joe Rudi, or Sal Bando), but that was okay with me. They were still Major Leaguers. In fact, my four opponents had 34 years of MLB time and hit an accumulated 143 homeruns between them. I know—I looked it up.

My exuberance over the one inning against the A's was short-lived, though. The next day I pitched against Cal State Hayward—not exactly a college powerhouse—and gave up seven runs in an inning and a third. That seemed to be the story of my college baseball career.

Upon graduation in 1973, I was able to stay involved in baseball by hooking on as the assistant coach of the Cal junior varsity team. In 1975, I moved over to St. Mary's College as the varsity pitching coach and then was hired back at Cal by head coach Jackie Jensen in 1976, where I worked as the pitching coach through 1977.

Jensen, nicknamed the "Golden Boy", is arguably the greatest athlete in the history of the university. He was an All-American running back for the Golden Bears and led them to the Rose Bowl in 1948. He also excelled in baseball and led Cal to the first ever College World Series in 1947, defeating the squad from Yale that featured a first baseman named George Bush. Jensen went on to a terrific career in the Major Leagues, playing eleven seasons, mostly with the Boston Red Sox. He was named the Most Valuable Player of the American League in 1958.

Bob Milano took over as Cal's baseball coach in 1978. He led the Golden Bears to College World Series appearances in 1980, 1988, and 1992, and he retired in 2000 with the most victories in the history of the program. In 2010 he was inducted into the Hall of Fame of the American Baseball Coaches Association.

*Here I am pictured with Head Coach Jackie Jensen and main Assistant
Coach Bob Milano.*

In November 1976, my world was about to change. I had
read a very popular novel by James Clavell called *SHOGUN*,
which made me determined to go to Asia. One night I was
at a Berkeley watering hole called Kips with a former Cal
teammate named Neil Cummings. A third-year law student,
Cummings was about to take the State Bar of California exam.
After about three pitchers of beer, I mentioned Clavell's novel
and how much I wanted to see Asia, to which Neil responded
that he had the same desire, and so we decided to form a
baseball team and play games on the other side of the pond.
The more we talked, the more exciting (and feasible) the idea
became. The only problem was that we had no idea how we
were going to pull it off.

A couple of breaks came our way, though. I was taking graduate classes at San Francisco State University, and one of my classmates was a gentleman named Liu Chi. It turned out that Liu Chi had a friend who was a big wig with the Taiwan Baseball Association—a man who had the pull to make arrangements for our proposed team in Taiwan. On top of that piece of good fortune, George Wolfman, the former Cal baseball coach, introduced Neil and me to a man with terrific contacts in Japan and Hawaii: Cappy Harada. After working with the San Francisco Giants, Harada had also done promotional work for the Major League Baseball Commissioner's office in the United States and Japan.

After numerous meetings with Liu Chi and Cappy, a plan was put into motion. We would play a couple of games in Hawaii and then head on to Taipei for a couple of weeks; after that, we would finish our competition with games in Osaka and the Tokyo area before returning to San Francisco. Through their contacts, Cappy was going to arrange airfares and lodging in Hawaii and Japan while Liu Chi was to do the same in Taiwan. With their pull, the total cost for each player to make the trip was estimated to be approximately five hundred dollars. It was a hell of a deal.

Of course, we had to put together a team, which turned out to be more difficult than we anticipated. Most of the good players Neil and I spoke to either were going off to play in summer collegiate leagues or, more realistically, thought we were loco.

Eventually, we were able to convince seventeen guys that we were for real, and our roster consisted of nine players from Cal, with the majority of the remaining players from various schools such as Cal Poly, UC Davis, and Santa Clara University. There were also a couple of guys who didn't play anywhere—we just needed bodies to make the plan work.

Neil and I had taken it for granted that we would call ourselves the Cal Bears and that the university would embrace and endorse our endeavor. However, we found out we were wrong when Dave Maggard, the Cal Athletic Director, wanted nothing to do with us, so we were forced to change our name. We decided to name ourselves the California All-Stars—boy, was that a stretch! Bob Milano, the newly appointed head varsity coach, felt sorry for us, so he promised us the use of Cal practice gear: old flannel uniforms from the 60s. Some were faded grey, and others a tint of blue. We didn't complain, though, because we had uniforms. Bob also threw in a couple sets of catcher's gear and a few used aluminum bats. While we were happy to have uniforms and gear, the truth is that we were a sorry sight for a team claiming to be the California All-Stars.

Throughout June and July 1977, Neil and I worked on details with Cappy and Liu Chi. By the end of July, it looked like we were really going to be able to pull this adventure off, and everything seemed to be in order for our August 9th departure.

Everything, that is, until the evening of August 8th when Cappy Harada called to tell me the dorm rooms he was supposed to have arranged for us at the University of Hawaii had not panned out. Great! For our first three nights of the trip, there was now no room in the inn. I kept asking myself how I was supposed to explain the situation to eighteen guys; for a while, the best I could come up with was something along the lines of "Gee, fellas, it won't be so bad. Maybe we can sleep on the beach." But then a light bulb went off in my head. I had become friendly with a young lady named Sharon Sousa, a teller at a local Berkeley bank. By lucky coincidence, she hailed from Kailua, a small city on the southeastern side of

Oahu. I called Sharon and explained our plight, asking if she had any suggestions. Promising to call me back, we hung up. Ten minutes later, my phone rang. Thinking it was Sharon, I quickly answered, only to find Mac Ikuma, the representative from Japan Airlines, who Cappy had been working with, on the other end of the line.

"I have bad news," he told me.

"Great," I thought. "First the lodging—now what?"

Mac continued, "The deposit you gave Mr. Harada for your tickets has not arrived yet."

We had collected the five hundred dollars from each player the week before and had passed the total on to Cappy, who was then supposed to get it to Japan Airlines to secure our seats.

"So what does that mean?" I asked, really dreading the answer. After all, we were scheduled to fly out of San Francisco Airport the next afternoon. Eighteen guys were going to show up to join me at the airport, expecting to have plane tickets—and a place to stay.

"No money, no ticket!" Ikuma answered, with no trace of sympathy.

Aghast, I asked, "What should we do?"

"Well, just show up, and let's hope the money arrives by tomorrow morning."

That was reassuring.

It was ten o'clock that night before Sharon finally called back. "I spoke to my mom and dad. This may not be much, but they said you could all stay at their house." Nineteen baseball players sleeping on the living room floor didn't sound like the perfect scenario, but at least I knew we would have a roof over our heads—that is, if we were ever able to get on the airplane.

On the drive to the airport the next day, I rehearsed over and over the speech I was going to have to give to the guys on why the trip wasn't going to happen, preparing myself for the biggest embarrassment of all time. "Sorry for wasting your time, fellas. You can go home now. We don't have plane tickets." I wasn't even going to mention the fact that they were going to have to sleep on a living room floor because I wasn't convinced we'd actually make it on the plane. Arriving at the Japan Airlines counter, most of the guys had gathered, some with their parents. They were all anticipating an adventure promised by me. All I could think was, "Please, Lord, let this burden pass."

But there was Mac Ikuma, holding an envelope with nineteen plane tickets—the money had arrived with thirty minutes to spare. With that, we were off and running with the players none the wiser to the near mishap.

The flight was unusual and fun. We basically had the back of a Boeing 747 to ourselves because it was what was called a "deadhead trip." Japan Airlines flew a full contingent from Tokyo and then basically took off empty from San Francisco to Honolulu, where it picked up vacationing Japanese tourists for the full flight back to the homeland. So it was nineteen members of the California All-Stars and fifteen flight attendants. And free beer. Enough said!

I waited until we were about halfway to Hawaii before I announced that our Hawaiian accommodations had changed somewhat. I didn't go into detail since I didn't have a solid idea of what they would be like. In fact, the only thing I knew for certain was that I had the Sousas' phone number and planned to call them when we arrived.

To this day I wonder at the ability of people to be so nice and accommodating. When we arrived in Honolulu, Mr. and

Mrs. Sousa were waiting for us at the gate with leis for each player and a bus to their home. These people had never met a single one of us, and yet they had not only opened their home to nineteen strangers but had also gone to the trouble of arranging for our travel around Oahu. Things do happen in life that defy expectations—and even explanation.

After three games, two practices, and a pig roast in their backyard, we had to bid the Sousas farewell because it was time to move on to Taiwan.

On our way to Taiwan, though, we had a one-night layover in Japan. From our hotel in Tokyo, I placed a call to Liu Chi, who was waiting in Taipei for our arrival. "Everything here is ready for you," he said. "I will meet you at the airport. I have notified some press people about your team, so there may be some there when you arrive." Before hanging up, he said, "Make sure you bring some gifts for the leaders of the Taiwan Baseball Association."

"Like what?" I asked.

"Go to the duty-free shop at the Tokyo airport and have each player pick up a bottle of Johnnie Walker Black and a carton of Kent cigarettes," Liu Chi directed. I thought it was a strange request, but I wasn't going to argue with him. At the duty-free shop at Haneda International Airport, each player purchased a fifth and a carton.

Three hours later, the California All-Stars arrived in Taipei, cleared customs, and were led into a special room. There, waiting for us, was Liu Chi and a contingent of press people, including television crews. Here was the young American baseball team, arriving to spread goodwill and their love of baseball, with each player toting a bottle of whiskey and a carton of cigarettes. It created a beautiful image—so beautiful that it showed up on the evening news that night and in papers the following morning.

The image we portrayed on the field echoed what was shown in the press. The California All-Stars were, in a nutshell, brutal. Liu Chi had gone overboard telling people on the Taiwan Baseball Association that we were a very good ball club, so our games were hyped up by the press. Good crowds, some in excess of five thousand fans, ventured to the national stadium, and they all saw bad baseball. Our overall record in Taiwan was two wins and eight losses. Steve Brown, a tall right-hander from UC Davis, pitched both the victories. Four years later, Brown actually made a few appearances for the California Angels, so he was a legitimate player. I still don't totally understand how he ended up on that trip with us.

The California All-Stars at Taiwan's National Baseball Stadium. Note the old flannel uniforms. Eighth from the left is Steve Brown.

Ballgames aside, the experience in Taiwan was awesome. Liu Chi had set up various tours, and we had ample time to explore, shop, and sightsee. And plenty of time to drink beer and hit on the girls of Taipei, which is the main reason I think most of the guys came to begin with.

Playing at the National Stadium in Taipei. The crowds we drew to our games in Taiwan and Japan were extraordinary, considering the talent we put on the field.

One of the most humorous moments came in our second week of the trip. A typhoon had hit the island, and for four days the California All-Stars couldn't go near the ball field. All the games had to be postponed, and we were pretty much isolated in our hotel. It was really nasty. The rain was blowing sideways, and the wind was howling, so there was no way we could take the field. On the morning of the fourth day, Liu Chi realized that we needed to get out, as the guys were going crazy being cooped up, so he suggested a tour of the Taiwan Brewing Company. Amazingly, all of the members of the team anxiously volunteered to go on this trip.

We bussed over to the Brewery, where we were shown why Taiwan Beer was the best in the country. When we got there, we were ushered into a private tasting room, all our glasses were filled, and toasts were offered. After chug-a-lugging that round, there was another toast with another round. That batch went down the hatch, and another appeared. And those rounds kept coming. While all this debauchery was going on, there was a little old man who made sure that the glasses, once emptied, were refilled. He scampered around the room, and once a glass was put down, he was Johnny-on-the-spot. Mugs were never empty for long.

By 3:00 in the afternoon, either the brewery ran out of beer, or they became sick of our mooching, and so we headed back to our bus. As soon as we stepped out of the building, we notice that the day looked a little brighter—and not just because we were tipsy and out of our hotel. The sun had come out. *Uh-oh!* The shining sun meant that day's game was on.

Three hours later, after warm-ups that were probably a bit abnormal looking, both teams lined up between the mound and home plate for the traditional pre-game ceremony, and I'm pretty sure our opponents could smell the beer permeating out of us. After the playing of the national anthems and exchanging of gifts (in our case, small American flags), the door behind the backstop opened, and out stepped the umpires for the contest. When the home plate arbiter stepped forward, I almost fell over. It was the same little old man who had kept refreshing our glasses at the brewery! All I could think was, "Those sneaky S.O.Bs."

I don't think it came as a surprise to any of us that we lost that game. And we lost it big time: The final score was 17-1. I'm sure we left quite an impression on the baseball fans of Taipei.

Dave Milaslovich, our catcher, enjoying the Taiwan Brewery. The man happily filling Dave's glass turned out to be the home plate umpire at our game later that evening.

Osaka was our first stop in Japan, where we only had one game scheduled. Keeping in stride of our losing streak, we lost 5-4 to the team from Osaka College of Commerce.

The day before that game, I was sitting in the lobby of our hotel when a well-dressed man walked up and politely inquired if I was the leader of the American baseball team staying in the hotel. My first thought was that he was a cop and that we were in trouble. They couldn't arrest us for being a bad baseball team, could they? He introduced himself as Steve Kawaguchi and said he worked for a Japanese sporting goods company by the name of Mizuno. He said the company had baseball products that they wanted to donate to our team. I thought it was a joke—obviously, they had not seen us play.

Freebies are freebies, though, so I rounded up the guys, and we headed off to Mizuno's main store and offices in the center of Osaka. And what a store it was—six floors of the most impressive array of athletic goods I had ever seen. There was a floor for each category: golf, apparel, baseball, running, etc. We were adults (and I use that term loosely) in a candy store. Each of the California All-Stars received a free pair of baseball shoes and a ball glove; those ball gloves were the finest I had ever put on my hand. And all this was for a few promotional pictures the company wanted to take of our squad because, in those days, an American team with their products had value. I later found out that Cappy Harada had arranged for all of this, and I presume he sold the Mizuno people a pretty good yarn that we were truly an all-star team.

Little did I know what that day would mean for my future.

After the game in Osaka, the next stop on the tour for the California All-Stars was Tokai University, one of the "Big Six" schools in Japanese college baseball. The schedule Cappy arranged called for us to play two games against Tokai and one against Meiji University, another one of the "Big Six." We then had four days off before bussing the sixty miles to Haneda Airport in Tokyo for the flight back to San Francisco.

The California All-Stars posing in front of the Mizuno store in Osaka. The man in the white coat in front is Steve Kawaguchi.

Or so I thought. On the bus out to Tokai, the representative of the Japanese Baseball Association casually remarked that after the final game against Tokai University, a bus would be taking us to the airport. I corrected her, stating that we were not scheduled to leave until September 3, seven days hence. "So sorry," she said. "I was instructed to take you back to the airport on August 31." And that was that. I have often wondered if the heads of the Japanese Baseball Association witnessed our pathetic play and made the decision to get us out of the country as quickly as they could.

One of our games at Tokai University. I think the kids sitting on the fence were waiting for some free baseballs courtesy of homeruns hit by their local heroes—of which there were many.

So, following our three losses (naturally) to Tokai and Meiji, we were on our own. Nineteen derelicts in Japan with very limited funds and no rooms. What were we to do?

I called a team meeting, and we came up with the only plan that our empty wallets would allow. We hopped a train to a small city at the foot of Mount Fuji, aptly named Fujiyoshita, where we spent three nights at a youth hostel. There was plenty of Kirin Beer and females from Russia, Sweden, Australia—not to mention Japan and the good ol' USA—inhabiting the place. The heck with baseball! We even spent a day climbing Mount Fuji.

All good things must come to an end, though, and on September 3, we pooled the last of our funds and hopped the train to Haneda. Fourteen hours later, when the wheels touched down in San Francisco, the adventure was over.

And so was my coaching career at the University of California. Jackie Jensen, the head coach had been fired, and I went down with the ship. Considering the fact that I was scheduled to be married three months later, I figured it was time to get serious about finding a real job.

At the age of twenty-six, with a degree in Physical Education and coaching as my only real job experience, that was a task easier said than done. I applied for just about anything I could find in the want ads—light bulb sales, training for a pest control company... You name it—I applied for it. My father arranged for an interview with his employer, Chubb and Son Insurance Company. Nothing there, either.

The low point came when my cousin's husband, Dave Laforest, a stock broker, arranged for what I thought was an interview with Merrill Lynch at the downtown Los Angeles office. "You would be perfect for this business. A natural born salesman," he told me.

When I arrived for the 3:00 p.m. interview, I was directed to a room where there were about thirty other people also waiting. I wondered why they were all there. It couldn't be for the same reason; after all, mine was a private interview set up by Dave. Right!

After a long wait, a lady came in and formally announced how the "interview" was going to take place. Each one of us was given a half hour to read over a booklet that was handed out, describing portfolios of make-believe clients. Then we were marched out to the trading floor and placed in individual cubicles with a desk, note pad, and phone. I had absolutely no clue what I was doing. I was just sweating and cursing Dave Laforest when, all of a sudden, the phone on my desk rang.

"Hello," I brilliantly answered.

"This is Bill Johnson," a voice on the other end responded. I recalled that this Bill Johnson was one of my fictitious clients. "What should I do with my shares of AT&T?"

His shares of AT&T? How the hell should I know? So I stammered out the only thing that I could think of. "Sell!" And with that, I slammed down the phone and walked out the door. Merrill Lynch didn't bother to call me back for a second interview.

Things were getting so desperate that I filled out an application at K-Mart as a stock clerk.

Then, one day in October, I received a phone call from a man who introduced himself as George Sheldon, owner of Curley-Bates, a company in Burlingame, California. "I have photos of your baseball team that the people at the Mizuno Corporation asked I forward to you," he explained. After I gave him the address, he politely inquired who I was.

"Just another guy looking for a job," I told him.

"The Curley-Bates Company is a sporting goods marketing and distribution firm," he told me, "and we are selling the Mizuno ball glove line here in the states. Right now we are searching for a promotion manager. Are you interested in applying?"

Interested in applying?! I was flabbergasted.

Sheldon explained that he was first planning to hire a new vice-president of marketing, and then he would get back to me. He also stated, matter-of-factly, that Curley-Bates was distributing another baseball product, a ball bat called Easton.

So I waited to hear back from him and grew more desperate. A month went by, and though I did receive the pictures, no call came from Sheldon. Calls I placed to him went unanswered. His executive assistant was very efficient—Mr. Sheldon never seemed to be in or was always in a meeting. December came. I was really in panic mode. I had no job and a wedding in a couple of weeks.

Finally, the efficient executive assistant, a lady named Daphne Gilbert, called and asked if I could come to their Burlingame office the next day. So it was that on December 9, 1977, after borrowing a suit and tie from my brother, along with his car, I found myself sitting in the office of Bob Lloyd, the new VP of Marketing for the Curley-Bates Company. After two hours of questions and meeting the other managers of the company, Lloyd said, "I've decided to offer you the position. If you accept it, the starting salary is $16,000 per annum."

I couldn't believe what I was hearing—that was more money than I had ever dreamt of making.

Then he outlined the job description. "So that the brands receive high visibility, you will be responsible for getting Easton bats and Mizuno ball gloves into the hands of top players. The sales force will need stories to push the products. That's where you come in."

Almost as an afterthought, Lloyd stated that I would have to go to spring training to sign the pro players to endorsement contracts. I actually had to get it straight in my head—they were going to pay me to go to spring training. *Wow!*

It took me about three seconds to accept the job offer.

CHAPTER

THREE

The Workshop

I was going to spring training, all right, but I had no idea what I was getting myself into or what I was doing. After all, I had never been to spring training and had no clue how pro players obtained their ball gloves. Did they get them from the club, or was each player on his own? And, of course, the bigger problem was how to convince pro baseball players that they should switch to a brand that was totally unknown to them—and a foreign brand, at that.

The one connection I had was Gary Hernandez, a former teammate at Cal; his brother, Keith, was the all-star first baseman for the St. Louis Cardinals. So I hit Gary up for Keith's phone number. When I finally reached him, Keith acknowledged that he had never heard of Mizuno, and, besides, he had a contract to use and endorse the Rawlings brand. He also went on to say there were basically four brands used by major leaguers: In addition to Rawlings, which was the most popular, there were the well-known Wilson, Spalding, and McGregor lines of gloves. Virtually all players in the big leagues used one of those brands. So not only was I competing with contractual obligations, but I was also pitting a brand new glove against established names.

It was George Sheldon who came up with a brilliant idea to introduce the gloves. Rather than simply going to the camps and handing out gloves, he thought we should actually construct them on the spot to the specifications given to us by the players. It was to be a factory on wheels. No one had ever done such a thing before, and we were just crazy enough to try it. And so, we set a plan; I had exactly five weeks to purchase a motor home, gut it, and then install an industrial sewing machine and workbench. Extra storage bins had to be added for leather and all of the components that went into a professional ball glove. We also needed to have the Mizuno and Curley-Bates logos painted on the sides of the workshop—a little advertisement goes a long way. Finally, Mizuno was going to supply the real talent—glove makers from the factory in Osaka, so travel itineraries also had to be established.

In addition to outfitting the vehicle, I had to contact the public relations director for each club to seek permission to bring the workshop into their respective camps. The work was non-stop for thirty-five days.

Finally, on February 14, 1978, all was ready to go. In six days I drove from San Francisco to Ft. Lauderdale, Florida, where I picked up the six glove technicians on the 20th, including Yoshi Tsubota, Mizuno's master craftsman.

We were ready for the big day on February 21, our first camp. The World Champion New York Yankees, to boot! I was fired up, and as we pulled up to the Yankee facility early in the morning, my heart was pounding. There was only one problem—no one was there. I had contacted the Yankees, and, yes, they had given me permission to come in on "opening day." What I didn't know was that "opening day" actually meant "reporting day." In other words, there was to be no workout on the field. The players simply checked in and left. We were off to a rip-roaring start—a workshop for gloves but no players to sell them to. The technicians looked at me like I was the fool on the hill.

Rome wasn't made in a day, though, so I stuck it out and twenty-four hours later, the Mizuno Baseball Workshop made its debut. A new ball glove company was in the game. And the new concept was a hit with the players. No company had ever offered a service like this: building a unique ball glove, right on the spot, from scratch to specifications in three hours. The player would submit his order and come back after the workout to find his custom glove ready to go. They were amazed.

The Baseball Workshop, with Bob Lloyd and George Sheldon.

Therein laid the rub, though. Not many of the gloves were actually custom-made from scratch. The truth is, the player was initially shown a finished sample we had on display.

He then requested modifications, such as a different web, less padding in the heel, things of that nature. It was really a matter of adding or subtracting parts on gloves that were already 90% completed and sitting in our storage bins. After the player left for his workout, one of the technicians pulled out the correct sample and completed the modifications, usually in about thirty minutes. Then, another technician heat-stamped the player's name on the glove, and it was done. The players just ate it up!

The Workshop was a huge draw for the Major League players, as was shown by members of the Chicago White Sox. Number 26 is Jim Hughes, who went on to have a stellar career working for Rawlings Sporting Goods—one of Easton's top competitors.

The public relations weren't just for the players—the workshop was a hit with the press, too. After all, how many of the same story lines can a reporter write about the players and the team? The workshop offered a whole new twist, and for them we manufactured a glove from scratch. Normally, while the team was out on the field, the scribes hung out in the workshop, munching on our hot dogs, chips, soft drinks, and, yes, beer. Having a workshop in a motor home meant we were equipped with a refrigerator and a stove. There is nothing more appeasing to a member of the press than free food and drink. So the coverage, both in newspapers and television, was terrific! Each night, when we checked into our new hotel, I called the local press to invite them out to our factory on wheels. Many thought I was crazy, but when they came out the next morning, we gave them a hell of a story—along with a free glove and a belly full of the best tube steaks in camp. In return, we received free press. It was a great trade-off.

The Mizuno Baseball Workshop was a hug media hit. With the technicians working on the gloves, I'm being interviewed by a station in West Palm Beach at the Braves camp.

Giving the players free ball gloves was one thing; getting to use them was quite another. Keith Hernandez was right—almost every player in the big league camps already had a glove deal. We were able to sign a few veteran players, most notably Dusty Baker of the Dodgers and Bobby Valentine of the Mets, but that was it. Most of the guys we ended up working with were players on the forty-man roster that were slated to start the season in the minor leagues. These were names that did not mean much at the time, but they sure did later. We worked with players like Bob Welch, Dave Stewart, Brian Doyle, Ed Farmer, and John Tudor.

The first Major League players we were able to sign to Mizuno contracts: Dusty Baker of the Dodgers and Bobby Valentine of the Mets.

Even though we only signed a few legitimate major league players coming out of spring training, one would have thought Mizuno was the hottest brand on the planet by listening to our PR propaganda. Some of our competitors were not so impressed. Frank Torre, former major leaguer and vice-president of Rawlings Sporting Goods, told Bob Chick of the *St. Petersburg Independent*, "I don't feel they [Mizuno] are any competition." He would eat those words later.

Spring training ended for us when we ran out of ball gloves, but the odyssey of the Mizuno Baseball Workshop did not end there. Five of the technicians left for Japan at the end of March, but one, Tak Yano, stayed with me for part two of the workshop—a tour of the United States with calls on retailers around the country. The plan was simple. The Curley-Bates sales rep promised his dealer that the Mizuno Workshop of spring training fame would spend an evening or afternoon at his store, with the promise that said dealer would stock the new glove line and place an ad in the local papers announcing the promotion. While at the store, Yano re-strung ball gloves (all brands) at no charge to the customers who ventured in, and like spring training, I called the local television stations and newspapers a day or two before each appearance.

We worked our way north, with stops in Charlotte, Washington, D.C., New York, and Boston, before turning west for appearances in Pittsburgh, Columbus, Cincinnati, Chicago, St. Louis, Little Rock, Dallas, Phoenix, and, finally, home to California. It was a public relations coup—and it put Mizuno on the U.S. map!

One particular non-scheduled stop was memorable. While we parked outside the Dodger clubhouse at Vero Beach in Florida, a couple from New Jersey wandered into the Workshop and marveled at the work of the technicians.

The man asked me if the Mizuno gloves were sold at Herman's stores, and I had to admit that I did not know. On top of that, I had to ask, "By the way, what is Herman's?"

He thought I was kidding. Herman's was not only the largest sporting goods retailer in the east in 1978, but also probably the entire country. He also happened to mention that they were headquartered in Carteret, New Jersey.

A month later, while Yano and I were making our way north on I-95 in New Jersey, we passed a road sign for Carteret. I pulled off the road, located a phone booth, and looked up the address for the Herman's corporate office. Leaving Yano in the Workshop, I ventured into the reception area, where there were seven other vendors waiting in coat and tie for their appointments with the buyers. The receptionist took one look at me in my t-shirt and jeans and coldly announced that deliveries were in the back. Not to be detoured, I told her I wanted to see the baseball buyer. Admitting I didn't have an appointment, I told her I thought he would want to see our factory on wheels. The next thing I knew, Carl Fink, buyer and merchandise manager, was following me into the Workshop where, for the next three hours, Yano constructed a ball glove from scratch. I threw some dogs on the stove while Fink and I discussed ball gloves, spring training, and a lot of other pleasantries—all while the other vendors sat in the waiting room with smoke coming out of their ears.

When we finally left, I found another phone booth and dialed up Bob Lloyd back at Curley-Bates. Inquiring where we were, I said, "Bob, have you ever heard of a sporting goods chain called Herman's?" There was silence on the other end of the line. No doubt he was wondering, "What has Darby screwed up now?"

"I just spent three hours in the Workshop with the buyer, and I think he wants to buy some gloves," I announced, proud of myself. Bob's silence was a pretty good sign that perhaps such a visit was not part of my job description. I don't think he was too impressed with my off-road adventure that I was so proud of.

Driving around in the Baseball Workshop was not always a barrel of laughs. Breakdowns were the norm rather than the exception, and filling the gas tank during the tumultuous years of the Carter presidency was always a challenge. Who can forget the lines for gas in 1978 and 1979? Scheduling could be a major hassle, too, particularly when a manager or sales rep arranged for a store appearance but forgot to tell me. One time Yano and I were in Sioux Falls, South Dakota, for a store promotion that ran from six to nine p.m. At about 7:30 p.m., the store manager told me that I had a phone call; Fred Adams, Curley-Bates National Sales Manager, was on the line.

"Darbs, there's a problem," he said, excitedly. I realized that whatever problem it was, it was going to be mine, not his. "I forgot to tell you that I arranged for the Workshop to be at Cook's tomorrow morning at 9:00."

Well, wasn't that just dandy? Cook's Sporting Goods was a huge customer based in Denver—600 miles from Sioux Falls, which was about a twelve-hour drive. "Fred, there's no way!" I yelled. "We're not even done here until 9:00 tonight, and clean-up will take at least half an hour. Forget it!"

But there was no getting around it. Cook's was a big account and had placed ads in the *Denver Post* and *Rocky Mountain News* and all over the radio. We had no choice.

Yano and I finished up in Sioux Falls at 9:30 that night and hit the road. I dove down to Omaha, then west on I-80 across the state of Nebraska. About dawn, we hit the Colorado border, and finally, with about 12 cups of coffee in my gut, we pulled into the Cook's parking lot at 8:45 a.m. with fifteen minutes to spare. Yano, of course, didn't have a driver's license, so I cursed Fred Adams across three states during my all-nighter.

The Mizuno Baseball Workshop was a staple on the baseball scene for ten years. Whether at spring training, the College World Series, a softball tournament, or retailers' parking lots across America, thousands of players and consumers had the chance to see how pro gloves were made while getting their own gloves repaired at the same time.

The Mizuno Baseball Workshop launched the brand!

CHAPTER
FOUR

Gimmicks and Gadgets

Over the next few years, we were able to sign up a few more players to use the gloves, and in 1980 the Mizuno baseball shoes were introduced. The timing was a bit off, though. Nike also entered the scene at this time, and they had a bit more firepower than we did.

The big news for Mizuno's exposure was the signing of two of baseball's all-time stars—Pete Rose and Rickey Henderson. Rose, of course, was coming off seventeen years of Big Red Machine fame and was arguably the most popular player in the game. Henderson was just getting started, with one year under his belt.

While the Baseball Workshop was still gathering some favorable press, the oddity had worn off. Newspapers and television stations were not interested in covering the "factory on wheels" anymore because it was old news, which left us in need of new gimmicks and gadgets. At our annual strategy meeting with the Mizuno people, held on the island of Kauai in November 1981, we came up with them. Our new plan was to introduce, for show, futuristic baseball equipment to the American public.

First came the concept of designing a lighter ball glove by putting ballistic nylon mesh, rather than leather, along the fingers. A glove like this could stop a bullet. The creative juices were really flowing, along with the spirits.

Still trying to be somewhat practical, I thought about a calamity that constantly occurs to outfielders and infielders on bright, sunny days—losing the ball in the sun. So why not build sunglass material right into the webbing of the glove? It makes sense.

Then things really started getting weird. Do hitters have problems getting signs from the third-base coach? After all, they have been getting the same old hand signals for a hundred years. But we'll fix that. Why not put an audio receiver system in the batting helmet so all the manager or coach has to do is punch a selected button on a transmitter so the batter and base runner would hear a pre-recorded voice saying "bunt," "hit and run," "steal," or "squeeze"? It made for a foolproof system.

What about the signs between pitchers and catchers? Maybe the pitcher has poor eyesight, or the lights are bad. Besides, aren't the runners at second base always stealing the finger signals that the catchers are flashing out to the hurlers? That, of course, would give the advantage to the hitter. So we need a small computer system that will allow the catcher to push a small button on a transmitter attached to his mitt to send a signal to a miniature receiver on the pitcher's glove. When the catcher hits the "fastball" button, the "fastball" light is illuminated on the pitcher's glove. The same happens for "curveball," "slider," "change-up," "knuckleball," or whatever else is in the pitcher's repertoire.

Finally, we came up with the homerun. Pitchers, of course, warm up before every game throwing in the bullpen.

When the game starts, though, it is a whole new visual experience because there is actually a hitter standing in the box. Everything looks different, which could affect the psyche of the pitcher. So why not build a system where a pitcher could throw into a screen that has the visual images of the team he would face that day? For example, if Bob Welch was on the mound for the Dodgers against the Phillies (remember, this was 1981), he could warm up actually seeing images of Pete Rose, Larry Bowa, Mike Schmidt, and so on. What a concept! Never mind that it would cost hundreds of thousands of dollars to develop and produce that type of technology—we were all about the ideas.

None of the products of our brainstorming session had ever seen the light of day, of course. But our Mizuno compatriots returned to the land of the rising sun with the mission to develop prototype samples that we could unveil to the press just prior to spring training and could be carried in the Baseball Workshop. They didn't have much time.

While the Mizuno technicians and designers were working their magic across the Pacific, we had to come up with names for the futuristic gear. The "mesh" glove and the "see-through" web glove were simple—they were called just that. The electronic gear would have to be a bit more dramatic for the press. In the same situation, others might have considered hiring a special consulting firm to lend aid in our endeavor. Did we consider that? Hell, no! Doug Kelly, our vice-president/marketing, and I went to lunch at a local Burlingame deli, and over salami sandwiches we devised the names of the futuristic, electronic baseball gear.

First, for the electronic helmet worn by the batter and base runners, we came up with the Mizuno Audio Receiver System, or MARS. For the communication system between the pitcher and catcher, we decided on the Mizuno Electronic Battery, or MELBA. Remember, in baseball lingo, the pitcher and catcher are known as the "battery." Genius, I know! Finally, the computerized warm-up machine for pitchers was an easy one: Computer Pitching Analyst, or CPA. The futuristic gear was set.

Sheldon had decided that we needed to engage a professional public relations firm to maximize our anticipated exposure, so the Richard Weiner Agency, based in New York City, was hired—over my avid protest, I assure you. Why did Curley-Bates need a PR firm when they had me? After all, I could call the press. Was I ever naïve!

The Weiner Agency appointed a man by the name of Bob Wiener to handle our account, and he immediately began spreading the word to the national press about the futuristic Mizuno baseball gear that was soon to be unveiled. Wiener also recommended that we hold a breakfast press conference in New York just prior to the opening of the spring training camps in mid-February. The famous Tavern on the Green in Central Park was chosen as the site.

This was all good but depended on Mizuno coming through with the prototypes. Without these, we were screwed. Faxes were sent daily, requesting status reports. December ran into January. Then it was February, and we were really sweating!

In the second week of February, Wiener announced that he was able to get me booked as a guest on the *The Today Show* on the morning of our press conference, and that all of the major networks were planning to come to the Tavern on the Green. These people weren't stupid—there was the possibility of a story, not to mention a free breakfast. Nobody in their right mind could turn that offer down. Tommy

Lasorda, the Dodger's outspoken manager, had also agreed to attend the press conference, and was going to go on *Good Morning America* to stump the futuristic gear. Of course, he had no idea what he was going to be stumping.

It was February 10, and we still had no gear. Mizuno notified us that the prototypes were ready, but they needed a voice in English for the MARS, MELBA, and CPA. So, we recorded Kelly's voice and air-shipped the tape to Osaka.

Finally, a few days before the scheduled press conference, the items arrived at Wiener's office in New York. It all looked great, and we were like little kids playing with the gear. It was really cool holding up the glove and looking at the sun through the web, even if it was impractical. And listening to Kelly's voice on the MARS was hilarious. Push the button and get "hit and run" or "hit behind the runner" in his strong Bostonian accent. It was beautiful. There was just one problem: The CPA was huge and all crated up. There was no way that we could take it out to see if it actually worked. That would have to wait for the NBC studio and the set of *The Today Show*.

At 6:30 a.m. on the big morning, I hopped into the limo supplied by NBC and arrived at the studio at 7:00. *The Today Show* was already underway, with Bryant Gumbel and Jane Pauley holding court. I noticed that all of our futuristic baseball gear was off to one side, and one of the Mizuno technicians was frantically, but very quietly, attempting to put the CPA together. It was a large contraption with a small batting cage and a computer set-up that had all these blinking lights going off. It looked impressive, but by the expression on the face of the technician, I knew we had a problem. During a commercial break, he came up to me and announced in an urgent whisper that the CPA was not working properly. It lit up but couldn't be controlled. Once activated, a picture of a hitter was illuminated on a screen inside the batting cage, but Kelly's voice over just popped up whenever, right out of the blue with "throw a fastball" or "throw a curveball." Or, even worse, nothing at all. Damn! We would just have to wing it.

There was a commercial break again, and I was up next. Gumbel came over, and we quickly went over the products on the set. He told me that we had to be quick because the segment was only going to be a few minutes. And it was obvious that he was most interested in the CPA. Swell.

The break concluded, and we were on. *The Today Show* was shot live, so there could be no screw-ups. Gumbel was a pro, and we blew through the gear quickly. When I tried to explain each product, he cut me off and moved on. He wanted to get to the CPA because it had all the bells and whistles. While talking about other products, I kept thinking, "Damn, I can't tell him it doesn't work. Lord, this is going to be humiliating on national television." When we finally got to it, I started to explain what it was when Bryant reached over to turn on the switch. I wanted to yell, "Don't do that!" but it was too late. Lights started flashing, and all of a sudden Kelly's voice bellowed out "throw a curveball." So Gumbel, who happened to be holding a baseball, fired it right into the screen in the cage for a perfect strike. Before either of us could say a word, another Kelly instruction called out from the machine. "Throw a fastball, low and away." Again, Gumbel threw the ball into the screen. He then reached over, turned off the machine, looked into the camera, and said, "That's really cool. Jim, thanks for being with us. We'll see you next year before spring training. And now to Willard with the weather…" And, with that, we were off the air. I was sweating bullets and felt like passing out. But we had pulled it off, and when I later viewed the tape of the show, it all looked real.

With Bryant Gumbel on the set of The Today Show. *I was scared to death since I knew the CPA wasn't working. Photo taken by Mel Nudelman.*

Meanwhile, Lasorda had taken some of the samples, sans CPA, over to the ABC studio and went on *Good Morning America* with David Hartman. He described the MARS, MELBA, and the other futuristic gear like he had designed them himself. No one on our end minded because his voice lent more credibility to the products.

We had pulled off the national morning TV shows but were far from finished. A truck immediately transferred the CPA to the loading dock of the Tavern on the Green, and an hour later we opened up the press conference. I was at the podium with Sheldon, Lasorda, and Monte Irvin, a former major leaguer, who was representing the commissioner.

The room was full of cameras, and I could see microphones with the logos of ABC, CBS, and NBC in the hands of the reporters. There was even a new all-sports network called ESPN in attendance. Again, Lasorda was the star, demonstrating how all the gear worked and explaining why such futuristic equipment was good for the game and why major leaguers were looking to Mizuno to enhance their performance, and on and on and on. Of course, it was all bullshit, but Lasorda was one of the greatest BS-ers of all time, so it was fitting.

That evening, the Mizuno name was all over the national news broadcasts. Even Louis Rukeyser, on his nightly show on the economy, gave us prime time coverage.

The electronic gear was a hit at the spring training camps, too. Every player that came into the Workshop wanted to see the MARS and the MELBA. When Ozzie Smith of the Cardinals tried on the MARS helmet and heard Kelly's voice telling him to "steal," I'm not sure whether he thought it was cool or I was full of crap. But while he was testing it out, a TV crew from St. Louis got it all on tape, and Mizuno received great publicity along the Mississippi River that night.

Flashing signs to Tommy Lasorda at the Tavern on the Green.

Ozzie Smith testing the MARS in the Baseball Workshop.

In April 1982, we had another chance to garner publicity using the futuristic gear. The San Francisco Giants were going to play an exhibition game against the Stanford baseball team at Sunken Diamond on the Palo Alto campus. Frank Robinson, the Hall of Famer and Giants manager, agreed to instruct his pitcher and catcher to use the MELBA system in the first inning of the game. He thought it would be good for laughs, and we saw it as an opportunity. Calls to all of the San Francisco area press indicated that many of the top reporters would now come cover what normally would not be a newsworthy event.

A few days before the game Kelly and I went out to the Curley-Bates parking lot to play catch and break in the glove and mitt in order to make sure the miniature LED (Light Emitting Diodes) were functioning properly. They were.

I arrived at Sunken Diamond two hours before game time and again tested the LEDs. They both lit up like Christmas trees. The press was out in full force, ready to report on this historic moment in the grand old pastime. This included Lowell Cohn of the *San Francisco Chronicle*, who was arguably the most influential, and cynical, Bay Area columnist. He could make you look like a hero or cut you to pieces.

Everything was looking good. Good, that is, until the Giants pitcher and catcher went to the bullpen to warm up and the LEDs didn't work. I was going nuts. No matter how much I tried or prayed, I could not get the lights to go on when the buttons were pushed. I looked over at Cohn and started to sweat. If this didn't work, we were toast!

Just then, Frank Robinson strolled out to the bullpen. Because Robinson doesn't put up with any nonsense, I went right up to him and explained the problem. I thought he would growl and throw my ass out of there. Instead, he laughed and told me to go sit in the dugout and wait for him there. Then he called John Rabb (the catcher) and Renie Martin (the pitcher) over and whispered something to them both.

When he sauntered back to the dugout, Robinson called the press over and announced that he was going to change the set-up. His new plan called for him to give the signals to the catcher via the LED on the pitcher's glove. Then Rabb would give the signals to the pitcher using the traditional finger signs. "I just want you guys to see how this works close up," he told the press gathered behind him in the dugout.

When Rabb squatted down to start the inning, Robinson, holding the pitcher's glove on his lap with the LED out of sight of the press, hit a button on the set. Rabb, looking down at his mitt, nodded his head and flashed the sign to the pitcher.

This went on until that half of the inning was over. Rabb jogged into the dugout, handed the mitt to me, and exclaimed loud enough for the press to hear, "That is really cool. It worked great!"

Of course, it never worked at all. Robinson bailed me out big time. He told the press what pitch he was calling for when hitting the button on the LED to transmit to Rabb. However, no light on Rabb's LED was illuminating. Rabb was simply looking out of the corner of his eye. If Robinson had his legs straight, the call was for a fastball. Crossed legs meant curveball.

Cohn's column the next day declared Mizuno's "futuristic" gear would set the norm in years to come, and the company, through innovation, was quickly gathering player recognition and market share.

To this day I still owe a huge debt of gratitude to John Rabb and Frank Robinson.

Manager Frank Robinson flashing signs to catcher Johnny Rabb during our exhibition of the futuristic gear at a practice game between the Giants and Stanford University. Robinson saved me—and Mizuno—from a great deal of embarrassment. Photo taken by James Higa.

CHAPTER
FIVE

The Bats

What may come as a surprise to a lot of people is that aluminum ball bats have been around for a long time. Little League first started using them in 1971, followed by high school and college players in 1974. And since then, no product used in America's pastime has created more controversy.

In the early seventies, Easton was not a major player in the market. In fact, there was no bat with an Easton label when aluminum bats first appeared on the scene. There were bats manufactured by Easton, but they were manufactured for a traditional baseball company called Adirondack. The only way a player could tell the bat was made by Easton was a little, and I mean tiny, diamond "E" on the barrel.

It just so happened that, at that time, the Curley-Bates Company was a distributor for Adirondack. George Sheldon sold both wood and aluminum Adirondack bats, with a particular emphasis on the wood sales to the San Francisco Giants. Then, in a strange and very shortsighted strategy, the people at Adirondack insisted that the small "E" be removed from all future bats. Jim Easton is a very even-tempered guy, but he had a ton of pride in the products his company manufactured. So he insisted the "E" had to stay. And that ended the relationship between the two companies.

Ever aggressive, Sheldon then worked out a deal with Easton to put EASTON on the bats, and Curley-Bates would handle the marketing, sales, and distribution. In 1975 there was a new sheriff in the world of ball bats.

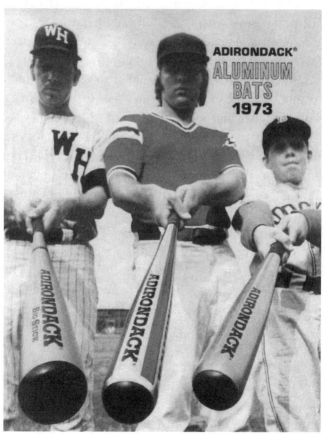

The early Adirondack aluminum bats, made by Easton.

But it took a while for the sheriff to have any real effect in the market. I had just started at Curley-Bates in December

1977, when I picked up an issue of *Collegiate Baseball*, a newspaper devoted to college and high school ball. There, plastered across a full page, was the headline "Worth Does It Again." In a graphic display, the Worth Company made it clear to the baseball world that their bat was used by more players at the 1977 College World Series than any other brand—for the second consecutive year. The ad listed the percent of usage, by company, with Louisville Slugger, Adirondack, and wood following Worth, respectively. Then came Easton. We were after wood bats! This was not good.

In the first week of January 1978, I went on my first road trip as an employee of Curley-Bates to attend the American Baseball Coaches Association convention, which was held in Atlanta that year. I had no idea what I was supposed to do. So, in my little ten-by-ten booth space, I just laid out my Mizuno glove and Easton bat samples. Coach after coach walked right on by. I was so frustrated that I finally rolled the bats into the middle of the aisle so someone, anyone, would stop. It still didn't work.

Just down the aisle, two booth spaces away, there was plenty of action in the Worth booth where the King of Promo, Paul Susce, was holding court. Known by every college baseball coach in America, he was the pied piper of aluminum bats. Every year he crossed the country in a Worth van, handing out samples to coaches and spreading the gospel about his company. He was full of B.S., but the coaches loved him.

He became my target.

Throughout the spring of 1978 it became very clear that Easton was not a brand of choice to many college or high school baseball players. Things looked really grim as the NCAA playoffs approached. The game was about to change, though.

During the final week of the regular season, Easton introduced a new bat to the market. It was called the "B-5 Pro Big Barrel" and was the first aluminum bat to have a barrel diameter of 2 5/8"; all previous bats had a maximum barrel diameter of 2 1/2". Additionally, the Easton engineers, using a special new alloy, were able to cut weight out of the bat, so the differential in ounces to inches was four. In other words, a 34" bat weighed 30 ounces. Most non-wood bats up to that point had a ratio of minus two ounces to inches.

Having a new bat didn't immediately create demand. Following King Susce's own script, I hit the road with my first stop at the campus of the University of Southern California. Coach Rod Dedeaux was nearing the end of his legendary career and had a hell of a team. After dropping off samples to the Trojans, I was off to the Regional playoffs in Miami, Connecticut, Alabama, Kansas, and Illinois, all in four days. I was Santa Claus in May, offering a couple of free bats to every team in the Regionals. I was baffled when some of the coaches wouldn't take them. A couple of them even ran me off, claiming I was disrupting their players.

I eventually arrived at Omaha's Rosenblatt Stadium ten minutes before the first game of the 1978 College World Series and witnessed a superb one-hit shutout hurled by Michigan's Steve Howe over Baylor. I also witnessed that there wasn't one Easton bat in sight. This was definitely not good.

Over the next few days, I saw that Susce was everywhere, talking to coaches, players, and just about anyone who would listen to his sermons. So I followed him. Every team practice he went to, I was there. The plan was to out-bullshit him at his own game.

Did I find success? Hardly. Players were not really hip to the idea of switching out the bats that got them to the World

Series, and coaches thought I was a nuisance. Mike Roberts
of the University of North Carolina cordially told me to take
a hike, as his players would keep swinging Worth bats.

I got a huge break, though, when Southern California
swept through the Regionals and advanced on to Omaha. A
few of the Trojans were actually swinging the new B5 Pro
Big Barrel model, which was quickly getting the nickname
"Green Easton," and the USC roster was loaded; almost the
entire lineup went on to eventually play in the major leagues.
They had names like Dave Hostetler (Rangers), Dave Van
Gorder (Reds), Tim Tolman (Astros), Chris Smith (Expos),
Dave Engle (Twins), Bill Bordley (Giants), Jeff Schattinger
(White Sox), and Rod Boxberger (Astros). Yes, they were
good. And, one by one, they all started to swing the Green
Easton over the Worth bat, first in practices, then during
World Series games.

In order for the Green Easton to get more publicity, they
had to win; the Easton sales pitch just wasn't flying with the
other teams. There was a scattering of players who switched
over to the Green Easton, but I needed USC to be victorious
for more to listen. The Series rolled on: out went North
Carolina, Miami, Oral Roberts, Baylor, Michigan, and St.
John's. Finally, the national championship game pitted USC
against another powerhouse, the defending champions from
Arizona State University, led by future major league stars
Bob Horner, Hubie Brooks, and Chris Bando.

While the College World Series has become a premier
television event today, and crowds average over twenty
thousand, this classic match up between the Trojans and the
Sun Devils was played before an audience of around eight
thousand people. And there was no television coverage. That
was to come later with the evolvement of a fledgling new

television concept called ESPN. For any advertising impact, I needed USC to win while swinging the Green Easton. Once again, I followed the lead of King Susce and literally became a Trojan. I attended every practice and made a point to converse with each player. I hung out in the lobby of the team hotel and even started to hang out with some of the players in their rooms, talking baseball and bats.

It all worked. Southern Cal, behind Bill Bordley, spanked the Sun Devils in the final game, 9-2. Eight of the nine Trojan starters used the new Green Easton, which gave Easton a huge win and the start of a new marketing campaign.

Two weeks later, in the World Series wrap-up edition, *Collegiate Baseball* ran the new Easton ad showing a bat rack with eight Green Eastons hanging next to one empty space, along with the headline, "8 of the 9 players on the NCAA Championship Team Swung the New B-5 Pro Big Barrel. Not Even Easton Could Hit .1000…" It was gorgeous!

A count of all of the at-bats during the 1978 College World Series showed that Worth was still number one, but we had cut into them with 33% of the total. We had gone from "behind wood" to number two and were off and running. All of a sudden, Easton became a brand in demand, which also had a positive influence in the marketing and sales of softball bats.

After that, the Green Easton just took off. In the 1979 College World Series, Easton's market share increased to 79%. In 1980, the University of Arizona, led by future Red Sox manager Terry Francona, swept to the championship with every player swinging Easton—a trend that would continue for the next eighteen years.

The 1981 College World Series was pivotal, for it was the year that ESPN first covered college baseball. The event had national exposure for the first time, which, in turn, continued the growth of Easton's exposure. Over ninety percent of the total at-bats were with the Green Easton.

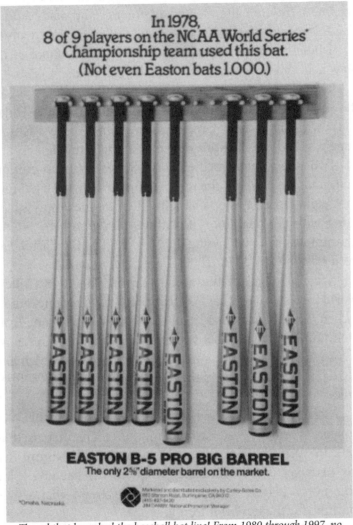

The ad that launched the baseball bat line! From 1980 through 1997, no other brand was used by the winning team in the championship game of the College World Series in Omaha—it was total Easton dominance!

The 1982 College World Series was memorable for one of the most bizarre plays ever seen, amateur or pro. It occurred in the sixth inning of a first round game between the Wichita State Shockers and the University of Miami Hurricanes. The Shockers featured a high-powered offense that was led by Phil Stephenson, who set an NCAA record for stolen bases during the regular season.

Stephenson reached first base leading off the inning, and everyone in Rosenblatt Stadium knew he was going to run. Mike Kasprzak, the Miami pitcher, lobbed a throw over to first, with Stephenson stepping back to the bag. He then took another lead, this time further off first. He was going—this was Shocker baseball. Kasprzak then quickly stepped off the rubber, wheeled, and fired the ball to first, and Stephenson slid headfirst back to the bag. Steve Lusby, the first baseman, dove to make the catch, quickly jumped up, and started scampering down the right field line, searching for the ball. Members of the Miami bullpen scurried about, pointing under their bench. Even the batgirls were up in the dugout, pointing down the line. Stephenson, of course, seeing all the action taking place, jumped up and started sprinting to second base.

While all this was happening I kept wondering why Kasprzak had stepped off the rubber. When Stephenson was halfway to second base, I saw why: There was the ball, still in Kasprzak's glove. Before anyone knew what was happening, including Stephenson, Kasprzak threw the ball to shortstop Bill Wrona, and Stephenson was a dead duck. Pandemonium took over on the field. Gene Stephenson, the Wichita State coach, and Phil's older brother, argued to the umpires that the play was illegal. But it wasn't—it was college baseball at its best.

Who was the brainchild behind this great deception? None other than Miami assistant coach, Stanley "Skip" Bertman, who, two years later, left the Miami campus to take over the reins as head coach at Louisiana State University. His clubs set the standard for college baseball, as he led the Tigers to five national championships over a ten-year period.

Skip Bertman on the evening he was inducted into the American Baseball Coaches Association Hall of Fame. Arguably the greatest coach in the modern era of college baseball, Bertman's LSU teams captured the NCAA Division One Championship in 1991, 1993, 1996, 1997, and 2000.

That play vaulted the Hurricanes to the College World Series title in 1982, and Easton's bat share continued to grow to over 95%, right along with an increasing television audience on ESPN. Attendance at the Series was growing, too, as seating additions were being made to Rosenblatt Stadium.

In 1983, Easton introduced the first 2 3/4" barrel baseball bat to the market, the "Black Magic." To account for the bigger barrel, the weight differential for this new bat was –3 ounces, which meant a 34" Black Magic weighed 31 ounces. Though eroding some share from its brother, the Green Easton, the two bats combined completely dominated the amateur bat market. So much so that at the 1983 College World Series, every player in every at-bat used an Easton bat—Easton finally batted .1000! You could say we had come a long way from "behind wood" in 1977.

The University of Texas, behind the strong pitching of future major leaguers Roger Clemens and Calvin Schiraldi, captured the Series title. One of the great performances in College World Series history occurred in 1983 but was overshadowed by the dynamic duo from Austin. David Magadan, another future major leaguer, rapped out nine hits in his first nine at-bats playing for the University of Alabama, a CWS record that still stands.

Coining a phrase from George Orwell, I can't say if "Big Brother" was watching in 1984, but I know a lot of fans nationwide were, as ratings for the College World Series continued to grow. Easton's market share at the event could not grow, as we already had 100% usage at the 1983 Series. It didn't go down, either, as we hit 100% for the second consecutive year.

People started asking me if Easton had an exclusive contract with the NCAA. Many believed that the teams had no other choice of bat. That was absolutely false. There were other choices—and good choices, at that. Worth was still a formidable opponent, as was Louisville Slugger. The difference was we worked much harder than they did. Easton promotion representatives went to every regional tournament prior to the start of the College World Series. At Omaha, our promo team never missed a practice. We made sure that if a representative from a competing company attended a team practice, our guy stayed after our opponent had left the field. A little friendly persuasion could go a long way.

Dave Magadan put on quite a show at the College World Series in 1983, right about the time that ESPN started to seriously cover college baseball.

We even found that a little body language could convince a player what bat to use. It was very simple. If I saw a kid swinging a competitor's bat during batting practice, I approached him with one of our new models. Of course, I inquired why he was swinging another brand, to which the answer was almost universally, "Just trying it out." I then asked him to try one of our new models. I never had a player say no to that request, and I handed him my Easton bat. I then held the competitor's bat while the player swung mine in the batting cage. I didn't just hold the competitor's bat, though; I leaned it against my crotch. When the player came out of the cage and saw what his old bat was leaning against, it was very rare, indeed, that he asked for it back. Besides, he had a brand new Easton in his hands. Just to be clear, I never kept a competitor's bat—I simply walked over and laid it by the team bat bag.

One time, while a team was taking batting practice before a game at Rosenblatt Stadium, I noticed a player swinging another brand, which was not good because a player usually uses his "gamer" in pre-game BP. Upon inquiring why he was using that brand, he told me his Easton Black Magic had cracked and he had no replacement. There was no way I was going to accept that, so I sprinted out to the parking lot, where we had a van stuffed with bats, grabbed a new Black Magic, and bolted back into the stadium. The game was about to start as I came flying down the stairs to the field entrance, and I did not see the metal bar hanging across the low door that led to the diamond. My forehead hit that bar while I was going full steam, knocking me backward and almost knocking me out. The "pop" could be heard throughout Rosenblatt Stadium. I was seeing stars, but, damn it, I had to get the bat to that kid. With blood running down my face, I staggered out to the field and delivered the bat. I think the kid felt so sorry for me that he would have swung Easton from that point forward, regardless of his bat preference.

Like I said, we took this job very seriously.

CHAPTER
SIX

The Gridiron

In the spring of 1983, Mizuno jumped into the football shoe business. "Jumped" may be the wrong word. We literally staggered into the football shoe business.

It all started when George Sheldon and I ran in the Bay to Breakers race in late May. Two hours later, George and I staggered into Stanford's Sunken Diamond to watch the Cardinals taking on the Cal Golden Bears. Standing right next to the press box, in all his glory, was none other than John Elway. Even though he had not played a down in the NFL at that point, Elway was one of the most recognizable athletes in the United States. He was an All-American who had just been the first player chosen in the NFL draft. And it was a controversial pick, as Elway refused to sign with the Baltimore Colts, the team that had selected him. It seemed that Jack Elway, John's dad, did not care much for Frank Kush, the Colts' coach. The NFL commissioner stepped in and forced the Colts to trade the rights to John to the Denver Broncos.

Sheldon was a huge Stanford fan (an alum of the class of '56), and seeing Elway lit his fuse. He turned to me and said, "Let's get into the football business." So we sauntered up to John and announced that we wanted to sign him up to wear Mizuno shoes. Of course, this created an interesting dynamic, considering that no Mizuno football cleats existed at that time.

Looking down at the two strangers in front of him, Elway uttered the only words that made sense. No, he did not tell us to take a hike; instead, he said, "Call my agent."

Mizuno footwear in the United States market was not a new thing in 1983. Curley-Bates started promoting and distributing Mizuno baseball cleats at spring training in 1980. Quite a few major leaguers went into the shoes in the first couple of years, including big names like Pete Rose, Goose Gossage, Greg Luzinski, and a young star just making a name for himself in Oakland named Rickey Henderson. A number of college teams were also using the Mizuno cleats, as did many players on the USA National amateur baseball teams. Elway had played baseball at Stanford and was familiar with the brand.

Football shoes, though, had not been in the plan; this immediate fascination with John Elway was totally out of the blue. The next day, when I was a bit more under control, I knocked on Sheldon's door.

"Are you sure you want to pursue this?" I asked. The Stanford Cardinal in George came right to the top, and he responded, "Absolutely. Get on it!"

I'm not sure if Elway's agent, Marvin Demoff, thought we were serious at first. John had always worn Adidas shoes while playing at Stanford, and the rumor was they were all set to sign him to a huge endorsement deal. Of course, the big gorilla, Nike, was probably going to jump in, as well. After a few phone conversations and a trip to his office, though, Demoff realized we were not kidding.

By this time the Broncos training camp had opened in Greeley, Colorado. On a Friday morning in late July, Demoff called and said, "If you have any interest in John, you better get up to Greeley right away and meet with John and his dad. And I mean today." So I busted into a meeting Sheldon was having with Doug Kelly, our marketing vice-president and told them about the call. Sheldon didn't bat an eye. "Let's go!"

An hour later, the three of us were on a flight to Denver, and after a ninety-minute drive, we found ourselves sitting with Jack and John Elway, two pepperoni pizzas, and a case of beer. Kelly brought a pair of "uppers," or shoes with no cleats, so we could set the correct fit for John. I'm sure they were nothing more than normal baseball shoes without the cleats. Amongst all the small talk, I could feel the Elways sizing us up. The whole time, Sheldon was sweating bullets that I would make a wisecrack about "the play," the dramatic Cal win over Stanford the previous November. John was never too pleased with the outcome of that game—after all, it kept him from playing in a bowl game.

Negotiations continued for the next couple of weeks, and the price tag for John's endorsement kept rising. Demoff played us beautifully, giving us the false hope that John had decided to sign with us and then, after we jumped up and down in anticipation, dropped it on us that Adidas was offering more, and we bit every time. We were at the point of no return: We were planning to launch the line and could not do it without a star with a big name behind it, and there was no bigger potential star at that point than John Elway.

Finally, with the Broncos' first exhibition game only a week away, we settled on a verbal agreement with Demoff. There was only one major problem to overcome—we still didn't have a football shoe. Kelly, whose background was in footwear design for Converse, was pushing Mizuno around the clock to get the initial Elway cleats to Denver in time for John's first appearance on an NFL field. We did not want the first historic pictures of our prize player displaying the Adidas stripes. And yet we waited. Monday... Tuesday... Panic was setting in... Wednesday... Finally, on Thursday afternoon, four pairs of white and blue football cleats cleared customs, and I was off to Denver.

Arriving at Stapleton Airport in the Mile High City, I was stunned by the exposure John Elway was getting. He had not even taken a snap, yet his mug was plastered all over the city. Billboards, posters, newspaper ads—his face was everywhere. I wondered what Steve DeBerg, the incumbent starting quarterback, felt about all of the publicity for this rookie.

After Friday's practice, I was given a press credential and access to the locker room and went in to fit John with his new digs. Everything was a go. Whew!

Saturday finally came. It was the first day of John Elway's professional career and Mizuno's entrée into the NFL. The Denver fans were absolutely going nuts. While Elway was the king of the day, the Broncos were treating me like a member of the king's court. After all, I was John Elway's "shoe guy." John Beake, the Bronco's Director of Player Personnel (and future GM), arranged for me to have carte blanche throughout the stadium.

In the locker room before the game, Elway put on the shoes and gave me a thumbs up. It was time to debut the Mizuno football cleats.

DeBerg, the veteran, started the game but had to endure 80,000 fanatics chanting, "Elway, Elway, Elway!" for the first quarter.

Then it was Elway time. Mile High Stadium erupted as number 7 ran onto the field for the first time as the second quarter started. And there I was in the private box of owner Edgar Kaiser, all because I was John Elway's "shoe guy."

A young John Elway showing off his Mizuno cleats.

The huddle broke, and Elway lined up behind the center. He took the snap, pivoted, and handed the ball off to the running back for a three-yard gain. The referee blew the play dead, and I watched in horror as John Elway jogged off the field, being replaced by DeBerg. Mile High Stadium went quiet as Elway took a seat on the bench and took off his Mizuno football shoes, replacing them with an Adidas pair. John then went back into the game on the next play, sans Mizuno.

All the eyes in the owner's box were on me, the "shoe guy."

At halftime, in the locker room, I discovered the ugly truth. When Elway took the first snap from center, as he pivoted to hand the ball off, the cleats on both shoes came out of the soles. I HAD FORGOTTEN TO TIGHTEN THE CLEATS! Welcome to the NFL.

All's well that ends well, though. Elway wore the Mizuno shoes in the second half and, this time, the cleats stayed in. I wasn't about to repeat that gaffe.

Two days later, Elway and I flew together from Denver to New York, where we had decided to hold a press conference to announce his signing with Mizuno. There was one formality that had to be completed. John still had not signed the actual contract, which I was carrying in my briefcase. Somewhere over Illinois, I pulled the document out, and John put his Hancock on it. The last piece of business was to have the signature attested. I asked the flight attendant if she would sign on the dotted line. Expecting a big smile and a willing partner to football shoe history, all we got was a frown and a decisive negative. It turned out that Steve DeBerg was her friend, and she did not appreciate our star client taking her pal's job.

CHAPTER
SEVEN

What the Puck?

One day in the fall of 1985, George Sheldon brought the Curley-Bates management team into his office and dropped a bombshell—he was planning to sell the marketing rights to Easton bats and the Mizuno products back to Jim Easton. In other words, he was cashing out while the getting was good.

Before the transaction could be completed, however, Sheldon wanted to obtain the approval from the Mizuno Corporation. In late November, a meeting was arranged in our Burlingame office. Masato Mizuno himself was coming, along with key members of his executive team. The plan was to meet all day, and then the whole party would head up to Candlestick Park for the Monday Night Football game between the San Francisco 49ers and the Dallas Cowboys.

"Get everything buttoned down," Sheldon told us, "and make sure the numbers are right. Darby, get all the player contracts in order so that they can be transferred to Easton. And, above all, don't screw up at the Monday Night game. Be on your best behavior."

George knew all too well what normally happened when we went to ball games or out on the town.

The meeting with the Mizuno people went great. The numbers were right on, and all our contracts and commitments were in order. It didn't appear that there would be any glitches.

After the day-long meeting, off we went to the football game. What a great game it was, with the Niners beating the Cowboys in front of a frenzied home crowd. Anyone who has been to a 49er game at Candlestick, particularly a Monday Night game, knows what I mean.

There were two non-frenzied fans, though. Kelly and I being on our best behavior meant no beers and no frenzy. We watched the game like two little choirboys. Everything worked out and the deal was completed. On December 2, 1985, Easton Sports was formed.

The transition from Curley-Bates to Easton Sports was exciting but left me with a sense of sadness, as well. George Sheldon was a tremendous man to work for. Through his leadership and direction, the company competed against traditional, established brands and was able to propel both Easton and Mizuno to leading positions in the baseball/softball industry. With limited advertising and promotion budgets, Curley-Bates had attained a nearly 90% share for Easton in the baseball bat market, while at the same time taking the Mizuno brand to the number two position in ball gloves and cleats in the United States. In addition, the Curley-Bates Company was instrumental in successfully marketing and distributing Mizuno running and volleyball shoes into key retail chains and specialty shops across the United States.

While we certainly had a lot of fun, Sheldon ran a tight ship when it came to business. It was true that we entered the football shoe business on a whim (see chapter 6), but once we committed to the venture, the planning was well thought-out and acted upon. There was a strategy to everything. To promote ball gloves, we targeted major league pitchers, because the Mizuno logo could easily be seen on television. Having quality footwear was crucial to top base stealers, so we signed, over time, Rickey Henderson, Tim Raines, and Vince Coleman, the top speedsters in the major leagues, to endorse Mizuno cleats.

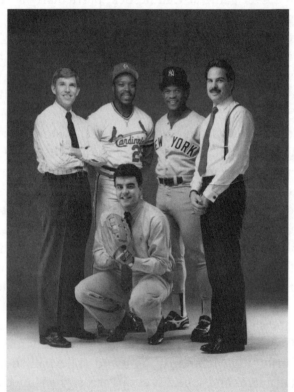

Here I am along with two of the best, Rickey Henderson and Vince Coleman, at a poster and ad photo shoot. Also in the photo are Peter Zavlaris (standing) and Steve Sanguinetti from our marketing department.

The Henderson and Coleman Mizuno ad.

The exposure built by these players created demand for the brand. To promote running shoes we targeted well-known triathletes, most notably Julie Moss, the young lady who brought awareness to the sport when, depleted of strength, she crawled across the finish line of the Ironman Triathlon on the big island of Hawaii. The event was seen by millions on ABC's *Wide World of Sports*. Sheldon always had great vision for the next opportunity and was very aggressive. I would certainly miss working with him.

The day after the transaction was completed, Jim Easton traveled up from Van Nuys, the corporate headquarters, to meet separately with Kelly and me. He wanted to welcome us to the Easton Corporation and, I think, to make sure we were staying put.

Doug Kelly and I had certainly met with Jim Easton before, usually at strategy meetings or trade shows. However, this was the first time meeting with him one-on-one, so I was a bit nervous going to dinner. I knew that Jim wasn't a big partier and was a bit relieved when he requested a beer when the waiter came by for the drink order. Naturally, I ordered the same, and, sucking it down rather quickly, I was ready to pull the trigger on another when we were asked if we desired another round. Jim ordered water with a squeeze of lemon. I quickly changed my mind and ordered a diet Coke. I could see that things were definitely going to be a bit different with our change in ownership.

In late May 1986, Kelly called me into his office to announce that we were going to enter the ice hockey business by introducing an Easton-branded stick to the market. This was a revelation—one I was not too keen about. After all, I didn't know squat about hockey. My only knowledge of the game came from attending a few California Golden Seals games when I was a college student and my buddies and I would down a few beers and wait for a fight to break out.

It turned out that one of Easton's top engineers, a gentleman by the name of Gary Felice, was a big hockey fan and had actually played the game in amateur leagues in Los Angeles. In 1981, he designed the first aluminum hockey shaft and obtained approval from the National Hockey League. Over the next five years, under private label, Easton was manufacturing shafts for well-known hockey companies like Canadian and Christian. Legend has it that the first NHL player to actually use the aluminum shafts was the great Brad Park of New York Ranger fame.

There were problems, though. First of all, hockey, like baseball, is steeped with tradition, particularly in Canada. Change is tough to institute, and convincing players to use the shaft was a tough sell. After all, Hall-of-Famers Gordie Howe and Rocket Richard didn't spin their magic using aluminum. Second, there was the problem with blades, which were made of wood and not manufactured by Easton. Getting a company to actually make replacement blades that could be delivered in a timely and consistent manner was a challenge. And third, traditional hockey companies like Canadian and Christian needed a good reason to put a lot of effort into an unknown product—a product that could eventually erode their core business, the wooden stick.

So that's where we stood when I walked out of Kelly's office in May of 1986.

After making a few inquisitive calls, I found out that the NHL players held an annual softball/golf tournament in Niagara Falls following the Stanley Cup playoffs. It was basically a huge party where some of the players let off steam at the end of the season. It also raised a lot of money for various charities, so it was all in good fun and for good causes. I ventured my way up to the Falls, attempted to meet some players, and sniffed around to see if anyone was interested in trying the new Easton aluminum shafts.

Alas, I was a dismal failure, primarily for two reasons. One, the players wanted to play golf and softball, drink, and chase groupies—not talk about hockey. Two, I sounded like a complete buffoon, a fish out of water. I had never played the sport and had yet to learn the language of the game. It was a very sobering experience.

I did come out of the trip with one lead, though. I was told that Tim Kerr of the Philadelphia Flyers had scored fifty goals the previous season using the Christian aluminum shaft. This was great news, except for the fact that I had no idea who the hell Tim Kerr was and how I could get in touch with him.

I started in the only place I could: I called the Flyers office and was routed to Joe Kadlek, the Director of Public Relations. "I won't give out Tim's number," he told me, "but I will give him your phone number, and if he is interested, he can call you back."

Fair enough, but I wasn't going to hold my breath.

The next day, though, my phone rang, and in a soft, laid-back voice, the caller introduced himself as Tim Kerr.

"Mr. Kerr, thanks for calling me. I want to talk to you about the new Easton aluminum shaft," I practically screamed into the phone.

To be clear, I expected the proverbial pro baseball player answer of "call my agent." But Kerr simply said, "OK, that's cool." I almost choked on my phone cord. I then made the next bold move. "Tim, I would like to come to Philadelphia to talk to you about a contract."

His answer nearly knocked me off my chair. "That's great. Let me know when you are coming, and I'll pick you up at the airport." Wow, what a sport!

Before I could meet with Kerr, though, I needed a course in hockey stickism. So, the next day, I flew down to Van Nuys to take a course from the stick wizard, Gary Felice. In two hours, he gave me a lesson in curves, flex-points, stiffness, lies, and just about everything one could want to know about a hockey stick. Believe me, a hockey stick is a far cry from a two-by-four.

Two days later, after drafting up a contract proposal, I boarded a flight to Philadelphia. After I landed and made my way to baggage claim, I looked outside; standing right next to his Porsche was Tim Kerr.

Tim Kerr is a bear of a man but extremely soft-spoken. After the normal introductions, we hopped into his car and headed off to one of his favorite restaurants/watering holes in the city. Within fifteen minutes, I swear we had become the best of friends. We ordered a couple of beers and chatted. Then another round, followed by another. After about five beers, I thought it would be wise to perhaps discuss the reason for my trip before the beers made me forget why I was there in the first place.

I opened with, "Tim, let me tell you about our new line of sticks," and then went into a discourse, trying to regurgitate everything Gary Felice had drummed into my head. About thirty seconds into my lecture, Kerr waved his hand and laughed. "Jim, can I ask you a question?" When I nodded, he said, "Have you ever played hockey?"

Uh-oh, I was busted… and didn't know what to say. I thought about lying to him but thought that would put me in an even more embarrassing situation. "No, Tim, I never have," I quipped. I thought I had blown the whole deal.

Much to my relief, Kerr asked if I had brought a contract with me. When I nodded, he asked if he could see it. I reached into my briefcase and handed it to him. He then asked for a pen, which I produced with shaking hands.

"I like you," he said, "and you came all the way from California to see me. I appreciate that. So show me where I sign this thing." I couldn't believe my good fortune.

Giving me a huge smile, Kerr continued, "But here's the deal. I'll sign this here and now under one condition: You will never, ever again talk to me about hockey sticks." And with that, Tim Kerr was the first NHL player to sign a contract to use and endorse the Easton hockey stick. It was obvious my knowledge had won him over. I thought a new nickname of Mr. Hockey might be in order.

Over the next year, a few more NHL-ers started to pick up the Easton sticks, most notably two of Kerr's Flyer teammates, Mark Howe and Dave Poulin. Howe, the son of legend Gordie (the real Mr. Hockey) had an illustrious NHL career of his own and is arguably the best defenseman in the history of the league not to win the Norris Trophy. Poulin also had a long and productive career and later went on to coach at his alma mater, Notre Dame.

It was at the NHL Equipment Managers convention the following year that I really earned my reputation as a hockey expert.

This event is held annually at the conclusion of the season and is similar to all trade shows. Vendors set up their booths and extol the virtues of their respective products. In this case, it was me attempting to tell the experts that aluminum shafts were the best things since sliced bread.

My big opportunity came when there was a break between their meetings, and about ten of the equipment managers were in the Easton booth. Seizing the moment, I held a shaft with a blade already attached and loudly notified my captivated audience that I was going to show them just how easily a blade, when broken, could be removed from the shaft and replaced. It was a real Barnum and Bailey act, and I was ready for them all to gather around for a short presentation.

Standing in the middle of my audience, I methodically held up a heat gun to the joint where the blade hozel entered the shaft. This was to melt the glue, which held the blade in place. Theoretically, once heated up, the blade, with a little pull, should slide right out.

After about a minute, I put the heat gun down, smiled to my new customers, and pulled on the blade. Nothing. I gave it another tug, but it wouldn't budge. This brought a few snickers from the crowd, along with some nervous laughter.

I grabbed the gun again, and this time there was not going to be a mistake. I was going to heat that sucker up and good! I blasted the joint again, heat directly on the aluminum, and got it blistering hot. Laying the gun down, I grabbed the wood blade and put the fingers of my other hand around the aluminum shaft, and… "AYGHHH!" I burned the flesh right off the inside of my fingers.

This was quickly becoming a real show. The equipment managers had never seen anything quite like this exhibition, and they didn't even have to pay extra for it. More of the guys, hearing me howl in pain, came over to see what was drawing so much attention. The audience around me had swelled to about thirty.

Now, I have a bit of pride, so there was no way that I was going to give up. That blade was coming out, come hell or high water. So I put the heat to the shaft again, and when I saw the glue at the hozel starting to ooze, I was ready. This time, though, I put on a glove. Taking hold of the blade and shaft, I gave a mighty tug. Whap! The blade came exploding out, along with flying glue, which splattered everyone standing around me. The blade ended up stuck to my tie, glued there for everyone to see. Mr. Hockey had struck again.

It was the end of my tie but was certainly one hell of a memorable demonstration. One for the records, in fact. I wanted to dig a hole right there and bury myself. In the long run, though, it actually helped. Many of the equipment managers felt sorry for me and later tried to help me out by supporting me and welcoming me into their locker rooms. I guess that goes to show that you never know what's going to happen—even if it initially doesn't work.

CHAPTER EIGHT

Hockey Stars

The acceptance of the aluminum hockey shaft was not instantaneous, even though some key players started to use them in NHL competition. Tim Kerr scored his customary fifty goals, which was a tremendous sales story, and in May of 1987, there was a terrific shot of Mark Howe on the cover of Sports Illustrated with the Easton stick prominent in his hands. The only problem was that Howe was skidding on his belly in the picture, while Wayne Gretzky was skating right by him with his Titan stick just as prominent. Of course, the headline on the cover was "The Great Gretzky." It wasn't perfect, but beggars can't be choosers.

We needed a breakthrough player, a star who would shock the hockey world by switching to aluminum sticks. We just didn't know who that would be. Obviously, Gretzky was the ideal target. However, he was tied up with Titan, and word on the street was that he was so finicky about his equipment that he would never change.

Then one day I received a call from John Pagatto, the vice-president of sales for our subsidiary company in Canada, who asked, "Darbs, would we have an interest in talking to Mario Lemieux of the Pittsburgh Penguins?"

Would we?

Apparently Pagatto and Super Mario had been friends for a long time, from their early days in Montreal. So, I told John to, yes, by all means, see if a meeting could be arranged.

I was soon on a flight to Pittsburgh, where, along with Pagatto, we drove over to the Penguins practice rink. Following the workout, I was introduced to Mario, and the three of us drove over to a coffee shop to have lunch and chat. I was envisioning another Tim Kerr negotiation and had the contract ready to go.

Mario turned out to be a great guy, who was very friendly and talkative. And that's what we did. We talked, and talked… and talked. Finally, Mario invited us over to his condo so we could talk some more.

Entering his abode, Mario introduced us to his lovely fiancée, Natalie, and asked us if we would like to have a drink, which I naturally accepted. So he went into the kitchen, pulled out three huge glasses, and made up a concoction that I had never heard of—something called a New England Iced Tea.

Our conversation continued, and a second round was called for. And a third. Then Mario jumped up to show us his newest, greatest toy. He pulled out a little box with a bunch of wires, hooked them up to the back of his television, and *shazam*! We could play video games right in the comfort of Mario Lemieux's condo. This was new to the rest of the world at the time, so it was pretty cool. Mario suggested that I play against John while he made us another round of drinks.

Dinner time quickly approached, so pizza was brought in. And the games continued, along with the rounds of New England Iced Teas.

The next thing I knew, I was waking up in the morning on Mario's living room rug, and my head was spinning. Needless to say, we never signed Mario Lemieux. In fact, I'm not sure we even discussed hockey sticks, but I do know that we had one hell of a good time.

Brian Leetch, left, and Jeremy Roenick, right, were two of the "young guns" who came into the NHL using Easton aluminum sticks. Next to Leetch is Dan Schuck, hall of fame slo-pitch softball star.

Over the next couple years, more NHL players started picking up on the Easton aluminum shafts. We weren't setting the ice on fire, but we were making progress. Young, future stars like Jeremy Roenick, Mike Modano, and Brian Leetch signed with Easton, and they all had dynamic runs in the NHL. Modano and Roenick both scored over five hundred goals in their careers, and nobody will ever forget Leetch's incredible performance in leading the Rangers to their 1994 Stanley Cup Championship. They also all had different personalities: Roenick was boisterous, loud, and outgoing; Modano was very smooth and had natural good looks that the groupies swooned over; Leetch was so quiet that it was hard to get him to say anything. The most excited I ever saw Brian Leetch get was at one of the Easton sales meetings in Hilton Head, South Carolina, when out on the golf course, he hit a drive down the right side of the fairway, near a fairly large rock. I watched him as he approached his ball when, all of a sudden, he let out a yelp and started high-tailing back down the fairway. The rock started moving, too. On four legs. I guess alligators get annoyed when golfers interrupt their fairway naps.

While our hockey business was steadily growing, we were still looking for the big star power, but that was about to change.

One day in the spring of 1990, Neil Hernberg, our hockey promotion manager, called me on the phone, all excited. "Darbs, I went out with some of the Los Angeles Kings last night after their game, and Gretz was there. He was asking me about our sticks." Maybe the road was open for us to find our superstar, after all.

Not long after that, Jim Easton, Doug Kelly, and I had dinner with Gretzky's agent, Mike Barnett. And the negotiations started, back and forth, back and forth. Each proposal was met with a counter proposal, which took us into September, with training camps opening. While the financial details were being bantered about, I was really worried about the product side of things. Remember when I mentioned that Gretzky had a reputation for being finicky about his hockey products? That's an understatement. One of the problems was that he used gear that was… a bit unusual. For example, the gloves that he demanded were unlike anything I had ever seen on another player. They had incredibly long cuffs and were bulky. And the pattern of his stick blade was not the norm. Maybe these oddities were part of why he was so darn good.

When we finally had what we thought was the right mix, I ventured down to St. Petersburg, Florida, where the Kings were set to play an exhibition game at the Sun Coast Stadium Wayne gave his thumbs-up on the sticks, but I was devastated when he skated out with a pair of competitor's gloves on his hands. After the game, he told me our gloves just did not feel right. With a week before the opening of the 1990-91 season, that was a comment that not only gave me little information to work on, but also certainly didn't instill a lot of confidence that we were going to get this done.

Back in Los Angeles the next week I must have given Wayne thirty different sample pairs to try, but none were just right. This cuff was too long; that cuff was too short. These fingers were too long; those fingers too short. The colors were not right. He was driving me nuts. I felt like screaming, "Damn it, just wear the frigging things!"

On the day of the season opener, at the Kings pre-game skate, I finally laid out three pairs of gloves for Wayne. Those were it—there were no more to show him. And if Gretzky showed up that night in a pair of gloves that didn't have Easton on the cuff, I was toast.

Wayne put the gloves on and, to my relief, said two of the three pairs "might" work, but there had to be some minor adjustments made. Minor adjustments? Damn! Where was I going to get adjustments made in time? I couldn't send them out to the factory because the game was only hours away.

Pete Millar, the Kings equipment manager, had an idea. He said there was a leather shop about three miles from the L.A. Forum that had done work for the team in the past. So I went roaring down Manchester Avenue, found the shop, and explained my plight to the manager.

"No problem," he said. "I can have these for you in a couple of days."

A couple of days? I could be fired in a couple of days. So I begged and begged until he said hc would see what he could do. I sat and sweated while he went to work.

An hour later he came out from the back room, confidently stating that the adjustments Wayne required had been successfully completed. So I scrambled back up Manchester, running a couple of red lights in my pursuit to get to Wayne before he left the locker room.

Wayne was just walking out the door when I came bolting down the hallway. "Here you go, Wayne, just like you wanted," I said, pleased with myself. He put them on—and then promptly handed them back to me.

"The fingers are still too tight." And with that, he was in his car and gone.

That sent me back down Manchester, where I begged for the proprietor's time again. Even though he had other customers awaiting his services, he came through for me again. Over the next two hours he stretched out the fingers, and I was on my way back to the Forum, thinking, "Please, God, let this work…" the whole way. I put the gloves in Wayne's locker and waited.

Easton's explosion into the hockey world came later that evening when the Great One himself came skating out of the tunnel with Easton sticks and gloves. A small California company had now taken on the traditional big boys from Canada!

The aluminum hockey stick took off in the early nineties, and the traditional wood stick was slowly disappearing from the ice. Then, in 1996, Easton was the first company to develop a composite hockey shaft, followed by a full composite, one-piece stick a few years later. By the start of the new century Easton was the most popular brand used by NHL players, a trend that has continued. Added to the sticks was a full line of gloves, helmets, skates, protective padding, and apparel. Easton hockey had arrived!

The Great One, Wayne Gretzky, signed on with Easton and switched to an aluminum stick—a move that forever changed the game. Flanking the Great One in the photo are Jim Easton and Doug Kelly.

The names of those who use the Easton brand is a virtual "who's who" of the NHL. In addition to Gretzky, names like Steve Yzerman, Brendan Shanahan, Brett Hull, Nick Lidstrom, Chris Chelios, Scott Stevens, Joe Sakic, Paul Kariya, Peter Forsberg, Martin St. Louis, Jarome Iginla, Joe Thornton, Owen Nolan, and Chris Drury slammed the nets with Easton aluminum or composite sticks.

By 2005, no player in the NHL was using a wood stick. Gary Felice and Easton had totally changed the game.

Steve Yzerman was one of the best signs I ever made for Easton.

*Steve Yzerman's popularity in Hockey Town earned him a spot on a
14-story billboard.*

An interesting sidelight to the Great One coming to
the Kings in 1988 was the explosion in popularity of inline
hockey. Of course, this made sense—Gretzky made hockey
very popular to young players, but in the southern and
western U.S., there were not too many ice hockey rinks.
Variations to the surface had to be adopted. More and more

inline rinks and arenas were established, and the sport took off.

And just as quickly as it took off, it died. But not before Easton and all the other major hockey brands had invested heavily into the growth of the sport. We sponsored leagues, associations, and individual teams. Unfortunately, after a few years, young athletes found other venues to fill their time, and inline hockey wasn't as popular.

However, during those years that the rage for inline hockey was in full swing, we decided to take advantage of the relationship we had with top young NHL stars to tout the line. In July 1995, we flew Paul Kariya and Mike Modano to San Francisco. There, we dressed them both in the hottest new apparel and equipment and made them skate down the Embarcadero from the Bay Bridge all the way to Fisherman's Wharf. It was amazing that no one got hurt as these two streaking NHL young guns weaved their way through the meandering tourists. There were a lot of dirty looks and verbal admonishments from those who were barely able to get out of the way. I've often wondered how irritated those people would have been had they known the identities of the young skaters flying by them.

Paul Kariya and Mike Modano taking a break from skating along San Francisco Bay in July 1995. This photo was taken directly under the Bay Bridge.

CHAPTER
NINE

Easton Sports Arena

In November 1987, a friendly name from the past called me in my office. Joe Safety had worked in public relations for the New York Yankees and Pittsburgh Pirates, but I had lost contact with him. If ever there was a PR guy, it was Joe Safety. Anyone who could put up with the mood swings and crazy antics of George Steinbrenner had to know how to handle all kinds of people.

It turned out that Safety had left the Yankees the year before and had hooked up with the Financial News Network, a cable television outfit based in Los Angeles. More specifically, Joe was in charge of programming for SCORE, the sports segment for FNN.

I was curious to find out what opportunities cable television offered, primarily to figure out a way to put Easton- and Mizuno-contracted athletes in front of a television audience with our logos prominently displayed.

Over lunch, I asked Joe how much it would cost to produce a thirty-minute talk show and was somewhat shocked when he offered up a figure of approximately three thousand dollars per episode. To my way of thinking, that wasn't much. Of course, I was not aware of FNN's per home reach, which wasn't very broad, but I was too intoxicated with the prospect of putting the Easton and Mizuno names on the boob tube nationwide to worry about the smaller details.

The idea was simple. We brought our contracted athletes to one of the FNN sets at their studio in Los Angeles; the show would air once each week, with at least two re-runs. Easton owned the rights to the footage, which I planned to use at sales meetings and trade shows. Safety offered up SCORE's Byron Day, a TV veteran (having previously worked in the sports division at NBC), to serve as the host of the show. Advertising time belonged to Easton. We could run our own ads, which at that time did not exist, or I had the option to sell the time in thirty-second slots with every sale reducing our production cost.

All I had to do was sell the concept to Doug Kelly, President of Easton Sports, and then to Jim Easton himself. In reality, Kelly was not a tough sell. To his credit, he was always very aggressive and jumped at wacky ideas, which explains why he was so much fun to work with.

Jim Easton and I were both flying out of Los Angeles International Airport one day, so on the ride to the airport, I presented the concept to him. For once I was prepared to back up my idea and was able to show him the costs, projected ad revenues, and potential viewership. He, too, bought the idea but impressed upon me that he wanted as much of the expense offset by the sales of the thirty-second spots as possible. He also wanted shows that featured all Easton products, including ski poles, football protective gear, wind surf masts, and aluminum arrows.

Once these approvals were obtained, Safety and I agreed to tape thirteen shows between mid-February and the end of

May, with a mutual option to shoot twenty-six more in year two. *Easton Sports Arena* was born.

Over the next year-and-a-half we shot thirty-nine shows. Byron Day hosted the first thirteen episodes as planned. I hosted the next twenty-six because, hell, it was too much fun to pass up the opportunity.

As for the ad space, I was able to solicit commitments from Mizuno for golf spots, Marcy for their exercise equipment, and even a thirty-second spot for a flying disc called Aerobie. It wasn't a lot, but it was enough to absorb about thirty percent of the production cost. On top of those ads, Easton produced their own ads for ball bats, hunting arrows, and aluminum hockey sticks to fill the other spots.

As "executive producer," my goal was to make the program interesting—and entertaining. More importantly, it had to have a positive message, primarily aimed at young athletes.

Getting professional athletes to take the time to tape a television talk show is not easy. I had an advantage, though. In most of our contracts, there was a clause whereby the athlete was obligated to make personal appearances on behalf of the company. The show served as one of these appearances, and there was the added benefit that the athlete didn't have to sign a bunch of autographs, which they all hated doing. It was really a win-win for everyone. The biggest headache was in scheduling, both for the athletes' time and the studio's time.

I kept my promise to Jim Easton. We taped programs with experts in all forms of sports and sports equipment. One show featured Stein Eriksson, the famous Olympian from Norway, with ski poles manufactured by Easton on the set. Byron Donzis was featured on another show, where he demonstrated the attributes of his innovative football pads, which, of course, were sold by Easton. Donzis had introduced his design to the market by placing a pad on Houston quarterback Dan Pastorini's broken ribs and then whacking the pad with a ball bat. When Pastorini didn't wince, well, you can get the picture. We did the same demonstration but with me as the guinea pig on the *Easton Sports Arena*.

My favorite shows were the ones filmed with athletes, and our list was impressive. Stars like Pete Rose, John Elway, Joe Montana, Dave Stewart, Goose Gossage, Orel Hershiser, Charlie Hough, Bob Boone, Roger McDowell, Steve Sax, Dusty Baker, Phil Garner, and Roger Craig were all featured.

As I said, each show was intended to be entertaining and carry a message. The following descriptions are some of my favorite highlights from the various episodes of the *Easton Sports Arena*.

●●●●●●●●●●●●●●●●●●●●●●●●

Roger McDowell

McDowell was the closer for the Philadelphia Phillies when he came to the FNN studios in 1989. A hero of the New York Mets 1986 World Series championship team, Roger was known for his tremendous sinker—and for being one of the greatest practical jokers in the major leagues. I asked what the best stunt he had ever pulled was, and his answer floored me… as well as the television audience.

McDowell always enjoyed the road trips to Chicago to play the Cubs in Wrigley Field. Most particularly, he liked to banter with the infamous bleacher bums hanging out in centerfield during batting practice. One day, while trading barbs, one of the bums yelled out, "Hey, McDowell, come up here and join us!" McDowell thought, "Why not?" So he hollered back, "Save me a seat," as the Mets headed back to the clubhouse following batting practice.

You can imagine the looks on the faces of the bleacher bums when, lo and behold, as the game started, none other than good old Roger McDowell came shuffling down the aisle. "They couldn't believe that I would do it," Roger recalled. "They kept ordering hot dogs and beer for me. I told them no on the beer, but the dogs were great."

The charade went on for a couple of innings, or about the time for the Cubs to start roughing up the Mets starter. "All of a sudden, one of the Cubs hit a jack that landed about five people away from where I was sitting, and I started to panic. I could just picture Harry Caray calling out 'There's a long drive to centerfield, and there's Roger McDowell. Roger, this Bud's for you!'"

So McDowell thanked his hosts for the hospitality, quickly scampered back to the Met's locker room, and switched into his uniform. Just as he slid into the bullpen, the phone rang from the dugout, ordering McDowell to warm up.

"When I was called into the game, the bleacher bums went nuts. It was a good thing Davey Johnson (Mets Manager) never found out where I spent the first two innings of the game."

For his zany antics, Roger McDowell will always go down as a fan favorite at Wrigley Field. And now you know why. You heard it on the *Easton Sports Arena.*

•••••••••••••••••••••••••
Goose Gossage

The Goose had a short stint with the San Francisco Giants in 1989, and it was on a trip to Los Angeles to play the Dodgers when he visited the FNN studios to tape the show.

One thing that always intrigued me was the ability of top athletes to play at their best in pressure situations. A closer on a major league team is in the pressure cooker on a daily basis, so I asked the Goose how he had taught himself to stay calm when the heat was on.

"It was the one game playoff we had with the Red Sox in my first year with the Yankees, the famous Bucky Dent game. The night before, I was so nervous I couldn't sleep. I kept picturing the game on the line and Carl Yastrzemski coming to the plate."

The Goose continued, "Well, the next day, here we are with two outs in the ninth inning. We're up by a run with runners at first and second. And, damn it, I look up and Yaz is coming to the plate. I was scared to death, and my knees were shaking. So I stepped off the mound to gather myself, and thought, 'What would be the worst thing that could happen?' Yaz could take me deep, and I blow the pennant. And, if that happened, I would be back in Colorado the next day, hunting. That calmed me down. I threw a heater on the outside, and Yaz popped it up to Nettles. Game over. I looked at every game in the same manner after that."

That, I thought, was a great message for our young viewers.

The Goose also entertained the audience with a story about his first appearance at Yankee Stadium as a member of the Bronx Bombers. The Yankees had signed Gossage as a free agent prior to the 1978 season and immediately handed him the closer's job. This move created quite a stir in the New York media since he would be replacing Sparky Lyle, a very popular Yankee and the 1977 Cy Young Award winner. Lyle wasn't changing teams; he was simply being passed by, which did not sit too well with some New York die-hard fans.

The Yankees opened the 1978 campaign on the road, where the Goose did not help his cause by blowing four saves in the first week of the season. When the club returned to the Big Apple for their home opener, the boo-birds were out in full force. During pre-game introductions, as the Goose lined up on the third base line, Ken Holtzman, standing next to him, reminded Gossage that it wasn't "Gooooose" he was hearing from the stands.

According to Goose, though, it really got bad when he was called into the game. In those days, a golf cart with a roof would ferry the relievers from the bullpen to the pitcher's mound. As Gossage came riding onto the field, Mickey Rivers, the flamboyant Yankee centerfielder, came dashing over and draped himself over the cart so the driver couldn't proceed. "Mickey kept pleading, 'Don't bring him into the game; don't bring him into the game,'" Goose explained, laughing.

Life could be cruel in the Bronx.

Even though he experienced a rough start, things turned out quite well for the Goose in 1978 as he helped the Yankees defeat the Los Angeles Dodgers in the World Series.

●●●●●●●●●●●●●●●●●●●●●●●●
Roger Craig

The Forty-Niners all-pro running back appeared on the *Easton Sports Arena* in February 1989. A very personable guy, Roger was outspoken and never at a loss for words. His answers to some of my questions were really surprising.

One that I put to him was typical: What did he feel was the best aspect of his game? Keep in mind that, the year before, Craig had set an NFL record by becoming the first player to rush for over a thousand yards and catch passes for over a thousand yards in the same season. In addition, he was also known as a punishing blocker. So I was really taken back by his answer: "I think the thing I do best is fool the defense on play-option fakes."

Say what? But he was serious. "Some backs don't sell the fake hand-off from the quarterback very well because they don't want to get hit. I take pride in being able to convince a linebacker or a defensive back that I have the ball, because if I get hit by one of them it means Jerry Rice, John Taylor, or Brent Jones is going to be open for Montana."

I had been a football fan my whole life, but that was the first time I ever heard an all-pro say his best attribute was fooling the other team. It changed the way I watched football games after that.

And it was all because of the *Easton Sports Arena*.

Doug Kelly and I share a moment with Niners All-Pro running back Roger Craig, who revolutionized the fullback position in Bill Walsh's West Coast offense. His unselfish attitude about how he helped his team win was refreshing to hear.

••••••••••••••••••••••••

Jay Barrs

Though his was not a household name like some professional baseball or football players, Barrs was a star in his sport: target archery. He had just won the Gold Medal at the 1988 Olympic Games in Seoul, Korea.

Jay Barrs had a fascinating story. To win the Gold, he had to go head-to-head with a Korean archer in the final round, which consisted of three shots at ninety meters (ninety meters is the length of a football field). Barrs and his opponent had to wait for an hour before the final three shots—an hour to fret about what could go wrong. And how did Barrs spend that hour? By donning head phones and listening to heavy metal music. With everything on the line, Barrs buried two bulls-eyes and a nine to capture the Gold for Team USA.

As dramatic as Barrs' story was, though, it was going to be tough to get an audience interested in a show devoted to archery target shooting. I figured a show like that required a solid opening, a shocker that would fire up the viewing audience.

No, I did not consider a live execution (well, maybe a little), but I did give thought to putting an apple on my head, à la William Tell. But I felt that would've been too hokey. Besides, why waste a good apple?

We taped the show in Encino, a suburb of Los Angeles, in the backyard of Jim Easton's mother. A target was put up, and Barrs and I were miked up for sound.

I asked him, "If you stand about thirty feet from the target, what are the odds you can put the arrow into the bulls-eye?"

"About one-hundred percent, unless something makes me flinch," he winked.

That sure boosted my confidence.

I stood directly in front of the target, with my head about three inches from the center. With the camera rolling, I started my opening dialogue, "Hello, fans, can you name a sport that has been around for thousands of years, a sport that requires balance, dexterity, strength, and, above all, nerves of steel?" On that word, Barrs let the arrow fly—right past my ear and smack into the middle of the target. I swear I could feel the feathers as the arrow shot by my head.

I can't tell you that the episode was a smash hit, but the opening was reality television long before its time.

Jay Barrs showing me how to shoot a target bow.

•••••••••••••••••••••••••

Dave Stewart

This story is not about the taping of the show, but what went wrong due to my insufficient planning.

The Oakland A's had just concluded a mid-week series in Anaheim and were flying back to the Bay Area following the

Thursday evening tilt Stew agreed to stay in Los Angeles so we could tape the show Friday morning, with the understanding that we would be done early since the A's were opening up a home series Friday night, and he had to be at the Oakland Coliseum by four o'clock. Those were Tony La Russa's rules.

"No problem," I told him. We'd shoot the show at 10:00 a.m. and then catch the shuttle from LAX to San Francisco International. My car was parked there, and I could give him a ride over to Oakland with time to spare.

Everything went smoothly on the set the next morning. Stew was a terrific guest, and I really felt like it was one of our best shows.

We finished taping around 11:00 a.m., perfect for catching the noon United shuttle to San Francisco. These flew on the hour, so I didn't bother to book reservations for us because there were always empty seats.

I didn't sweat it until we arrived at the United ticket counter and I asked for two seats for SFO, please. "Sorry," I was informed, "that flight was sold out." Huh?

"Okay, how about the 1:00 p.m. flight?" Again, the flight was sold out. In fact, every seat to the three Bay Area airports, San Francisco, Oakland, and San Jose, were all sold out for the rest of the day! It turned out that was the weekend of the Bay to Breakers race, and thousands of Southern Californians were heading north for the festivities.

Dave Stewart is one of the most kind, rationale guys I have ever met, but at that moment I was afraid he was soon going to face a serious capitol charge: my murder. "Darbs, I don't care how you do it, but you have to get me back to Oakland by 4:00," Stew emphatically reminded me.

This was 1989, before boarding passes were required to pass through security. So we went to the gate for the 1:00

flight to San Francisco, hoping a standby seat might open up. The gate agent just laughed, though. We were numbers 21 and 22 on the list. So sorry, Charlie. It was the same with the 2:00 flight. The 2:25 flight to Oakland was oversold by 25 seats. I even tried calling a couple of charter companies but was told the earliest available jets were for flights that evening. Besides, it would cost thousands of dollars, which would be a tough expense to explain to Mr. Easton.

We stood there like a couple of wounded ducks when a gentleman approached Stew and said, "Excuse me, aren't you Dave Stewart? You're my daughter's favorite player [the usual line]. Can I have your autograph?" With the autograph in hand and upon hearing our plight, the kind man stated he really didn't have to be in the Bay Area until later that evening; in fact, for a couple of tickets to an A's game, he was willing to give Dave his seat on the 2:25 to Oakland.

I began to believe there is a God after all. Stew made it to the Coliseum by 4:00, thus avoiding the wrath of Tony La Russa, and my life was spared.

As for me, I caught a flight back to San Francisco at 9:00 that evening, but I guarantee that was the most relaxing seven-hour wait for a flight that I have ever had.

●●●●●●●●●●●●●●●●●●●●●●●●

Byron Donzis

One of our episodes of the *Easton Sports Arena* featured an inventor named Byron Donzis. As I mentioned earlier in this chapter, in 1981 Donzis had gained national attention when he developed a specialized flak vest for Houston Oiler quarterback Dan Pastorini, who was hospitalized with three broken ribs. Utilizing a patented open-cell design, the pad was able to absorb more shock than conventional pads of the day.

Getting Pastorini to see, much less try, the pad was an issue, though; he was stuck lying in a hospital bed. As Byron later explained to me, he and an associate snuck into Pastorini's hospital room where the inventor demonstrated the vest by donning it and letting his sidekick belt him with a baseball bat. While Pastorini later stated that he initially thought Donzis was "some kind of nut" with his bizarre method of marketing, he did put the pad on and not only was able to play, but also almost led the Oilers to the Super Bowl.

More and more players, including Joe Montana, jumped into the Donzis designed vest, and the line was extended to shoulder pads, hip pads, and thigh pads. Eventually, Easton and Donzis developed a business relationship and, along with the pads, Byron was a guest on our show.

Of course, to give full validity to the line, we had to give a replay of the initial Pastorini demonstration. So I buckled up the pad, and with the camera running, Byron whacked me a few times in the ribs with a baseball bat. I didn't even flinch.

While this was a pretty cool way to visually verify the ability of the Donzis design to protect players, I always had the morbid thought of what would have happened if Byron had swung the bat and missed the pad. Now that surely would have jumped the ratings!

*I don't think Montana had to worry about job security, but it was sure
great that he wore our pads. This poster was sent out to a lot of high school
and college programs.*

•••••••••••••••••••••••••••

Mary Stacey

Timing is everything, and it could not have been worse
for me when we taped the show that featured Mary Stacey,

captain of the USA National Field Hockey team.

I realize that many sports fans don't give a hoot about field hockey, but Easton was just entering the stick business, and I felt it was my commitment to Jim to create shows that covered all of the sports that the Easton Corporation had involvement with, and Mary Stacey was America's best female hockey player.

I contacted Mary through the National Field Hockey Association office, and the only date that she was available was on March 4, which was a Saturday. Joe Safety said we could use the studio then, so we locked in the shoot time for 10:00 a.m. I arranged an early morning flight from St. Louis to Los Angeles for Mary and a 6:00 a.m. flight for myself out of San Francisco. That would get me into LAX just in time to meet Mary at her gate. Everything was set.

It was set, that is, until 10:00 p.m. on Friday night, March 3. My wife, Sarah, was just about nine months along, and that night, her water broke. She said it would be a good idea to head for the hospital, so we rushed out the door, hopped into the car, and sped off. And then it hit me that I had no way of reaching Mary Stacey. I didn't have her home phone number, and cell phones were non-existent. Even worse, I didn't have any home phone numbers for any of the FNN staff.

Three years before, in 1986, my son Michael was born after Sarah had gone through seventeen hours of hard, painful labor. Memories of that left her in no mood to listen to my predicament regarding Mary Stacey and the *Easton Sports Arena*. Nonetheless, the problem was real—this poor woman was going to fly all the way across the country, and nobody was going to be there to pick her up. Even more, she had no idea who to call, as I was the only contact she had.

Sometimes miracles do happen. Beyond the fact that the birth of my daughter was a miracle in its own right, she decided to set a record time on making her presence known. Sarah and I made it to the hospital at 12:05 a.m., and Sally Price Darby entered the world at 12:45 a.m. I was home and in bed by 2:00 and at San Francisco Airport in time for the flight to Los Angeles four hours later. What a night!

The show must (and did) go on.

•••••••••••••••••••••••••

The plug on the *Easton Sports Arena* was pulled after thirty-nine episodes for a variety of reasons. Our budget was shot, and I could not get enough commitments for advertising dollars. Doug Kelly also thought it was taking too much time away from what I was really supposed to be doing (he was right). The real reason, though, was that there just weren't enough people tuning in to FNN SCORE to warrant the time or expense. But it was sure fun while it lasted.

CHAPTER
TEN

Trade Shows

Some of the greatest joys and biggest headaches for a sporting goods promotion person are the industry trade shows. Usually, the promo person is responsible for creating the "hype" for the company at these events. Competing against big hitters like Nike, Adidas, or Reebok was, and still is, a continuous challenge, to put it mildly.

My first experience at an industry trade show was a disaster. George Sheldon wanted to have the Mizuno Baseball Workshop brought into the Anaheim Convention Center for the annual National Sporting Goods Association (NSGA) Show in October 1978. He thought it would be a good draw for the retailers to see the operation that had drawn so much press the previous spring, and since Tak Yano, the glove craftsman, was still in the United States, he could demonstrate how the pro gloves were constructed.

I contacted the logistics people at the Convention Center and worked the details out. The only real stipulation was that the gas had to be drained out of the tanks before I could drive it into the hall so that it was traveling on fumes. The day prior to the opening of the show, I drove the Workshop around the streets of Anaheim until the tanks were nearly dry and then headed down the ramp to the entrance of the hall. Now, I had done my homework and found out that the top of the large doors at the entrance were a foot higher than the roof of the Workshop, so no problem. No problem, that is until I heard a loud thump, followed by a resounding crash. I had correctly calculated the height of the Workshop but had forgotten about the air conditioning unit on the roof of the vehicle.

Whoops! Thank goodness the exhibit hall was air conditioned because that was the end of the unit. The Workshop did prove to be quite a draw at the show, but it certainly wasn't a great beginning to my career working trade shows and sales meetings.

The job of the Promotion Department at trade shows and sales meetings was to provide a good image for the company and to supply entertainment. This almost always meant getting top athletes to show up. While this may sound simple, it was usually a tremendous pain in the ass, and many times I was sweating it out whether they would actually show up.

Why? For the simple reason that the athletes hated making public appearances. Even though they agreed to such appearances in their endorsement deals, getting them to actually come was another story. Most of the stars absolutely disdained autograph sessions, and I can't say I blamed them. The majority of people who waited hours in line for signatures were collectors whose only desire was to take the autographed items and sell them. The athletes were keenly aware of this. They had to sit there for hours on end, acting like they really cared.

For the NSGA show in February 1984, held at the famous McCormick Place along Lake Michigan, our celebrity guest was John Elway, who had just completed his initial year in

Denver. It had been a humbling campaign for the prized rookie, but he was still in the national spotlight, nonetheless.

Accompanying Elway to Chicago was his brother in-law, Jimmy Walsh. A flamboyant character in his own right, Walsh had played briefly with the Seattle Seahawks and, at the time of the show, was part of Jack Elway's (John's dad) coaching staff at San Jose State University.

On the night before John was scheduled to appear at our booth, Doug Kelly and I decided to host a dinner with three buyers from a prominent sporting goods chain. Kelly made reservations at one of Chicago's finest restaurants on the South Side.

This was Chicago in February. A blizzard blew in which virtually shut down the city. While our party waited inside the Drake Hotel, I stood shivering outside with the doorman trying to hail a cab. We waited and waited, but the inclement weather kept the hacks off the streets. Finally, one pulled into the entrance way. I hopped in, and the driver, a small dark-haired fellow, asked me for the destination. Before I could utter a word, six more bodies, including the hulking forms of Elway and Walsh, came plowing in. Guys were piled on top of each other. The driver panicked. "Get out, get out! I can only carry four in my cab!" he yelled in a thick accent.

Walsh, sitting on top of his famous brother-in-law, was in the back, directly behind the driver. He reached over and grabbed the terrified man by the throat and said, "What's your name?" The answer was something incomprehensible, but it contained no less than five words and was obviously of Middle Eastern origin. "Well, tonight your name is Fred," Walsh screamed, "and you're driving. So let's go!"

So, with Walsh's meaty arm around his throat, "Fred" made an executive decision on the spot to proceed with seven passengers. The hell with the rules. Smart man.

On we drove, through deserted streets. Chicago was suddenly a ghost town. This was a serious storm, and it was freezing outside. But in the cab, it was dreadfully hot, and it stunk. After about twenty minutes, Fred pulled up to the restaurant, and bodies came tumbling out.

To this day I can't explain what got into me, but as I was shutting the cab door, I said, in jest, "Fred, park this thing and come join us."

Kelly had picked a posh spot. While we waited in the lobby, I saw many of the movers and shakers of the sporting goods industry enjoying their culinary experience. Then our table was ready, and we took our seats in the main dining room. Just then I looked up, and there was Fred, wearing his greasy overalls and a t-shirt.

I looked over at Elway, who busted out laughing. *So,* I thought, *what the hell?* I called the waiter over and asked for an additional place setting.

I'm not sure who was a bigger celebrity at our table, Elway the quarterback or Fred the cab driver, but there was no denying ours was the hit table of the evening. Everyone was staring at us and nodding. Fred was having the time of his life. He never did order dinner, but he didn't shy away from the appetizers and margaritas.

When we were finished, Fred announced that he had had such a great time that the cab was on him for the rest of the evening. Fred's instant celebrity status must have made him feel like *he* was John Elway, and he drove us around like he was right out of the *French Connection.*

At one stop, a couple of local heroes decided that they wanted to take a piece out of Elway—I guess they weren't Bronco fans. I could just see our star quarterback taking a shot to the noggin and falling on the ice, breaking something important. I also envisioned me losing my job. So I jumped in and scared the local tough guys away—or could that have been Jimmy Walsh standing right behind me?

At the end of the night, Kelly jokingly said, "Fred, the show ends tomorrow at 4:00. Darbs and I have to go to O'Hare, so meet us at the front of the McCormick Place with a twelve-pack on ice." Seriously, he was kidding. But, the next day, as we were walking out the door to hail a taxi, we heard this voice yelling, "Doug! Jim!" and there he was, same greasy shirt and overalls and, better yet, with a twelve-pack on ice!

Lord knows what ever happened to Fred the Cabbie, but he will certainly go down in my trade show hall of fame.

During the end of the 80s and into the 90s, the biggest sporting goods show in the United States was the Sporting Goods Manufacturers Association (SGMA) Super Show, held annually in February, one week after the Super Bowl. What a show it was, taking up the entire Georgia World Congress Center and the floor of the Georgia Dome. More than 80,000 retailers and manufacturers converged on Atlanta each year, providing millions of dollars to the local economy, most notably to the hotels, restaurants, bars, and strip clubs.

The competition between the manufacturers to impress the retail buyers was keen and intensified each year. The dollars spent on elaborate booths was, quite simply, absurd. While such lavish spending was expected by the industry heavyweights like Nike and Reebok, smaller companies like Easton got caught up in the hoopla. One year we had a second story built on top of our booth and a batting cage installed there so that buyers could actually test our newest bats. Of course, the idea was that they would come down and write orders.

Even more important than the booth was the image the company presented by the athletes they had signing autographs in their respective booths. Each year it became a "who's who" of what stars attended. In front of the Georgia World Congress Center a marquee daily displayed the names of the athletes that were scheduled to attend, along with the company they represented. It was extremely competitive, and the pride of the company was always on the line.

That meant the heat was on the promo team to supply the talent. Every year, starting in early October, we started to go over our lists of pros, checking to see who were the best choices to be tabbed for the "Show." As the Super Show grew, the star power of our athletes was also expected to grow.

Star power for athletes is something that I never have been able to totally comprehend. Some athletes drew huge crowds while others simply didn't. It probably has more to do with the value of the autograph than anything else. One year Dan Quisenberry came to represent Easton right after the Kansas City Royals had defeated the St. Louis Cardinals in the World Series, and Quiz had been the American League's top relief pitcher. But no crowds came for his autograph. I was crushed, and I'm sure Quiz was a bit embarrassed, although he never showed it. The same thing happened when we had Charlie Joiner, the Hall of Fame wide-out from the San Diego Chargers. Charlie's appearance was only two months after he had set the all-time NFL record for receptions. He, too, drew a sparse crowd. Go figure.

For the most part, though, when big-name athletes came to the trade shows, particularly the Super Show, huge lines wrapped around the various booths with people anxious to get autographs or get their photo taken with their heroes. That was another problem with the whole concept—people stood in front of the booth and the line wrapped clear around to the other side, effectively blocking the entrance to buyers who had actually come to see what was new and to perhaps even provide some business. Another problem was shutting down the line of autograph seekers. We tried to time it so that the last person in line was getting to the athlete just as the clock hit the time the autograph session was scheduled to end. Normally, with about a half hour to go, I assigned one of our staff to go place themselves at the end of the line and tell people no one behind him would get an autograph, which was fine until some 6'5" dude got in line behind him.

Brett Hull at the Easton booth at the National Sporting Goods Association's trade show in 1993. Brett was all smiles in this photo but, like most athletes, was not a big fan of trade shows. Doug Kelly and Neil Hernberg, our promotion manager, are also in the shot.

Trying to time everything was an inexact science. Each athlete was different. For example, with Pete Rose it was very easy. You see, Rose would always come into town the night before his scheduled appearance. He normally told me to bring the items we were supplying for him to autograph up to his room, and there he signed his name to each one. Then, the next day at the show, the autograph seekers just shuffled by the table, and Rose handed them the poster or picture he had signed the night before. Half the time he didn't even look up. Bing, bong, bang—and gone! That line was always easy to time.

On the other hand, there were guys like NHL star Jeremy Roenick, who were so friendly and outgoing that they would talk to every person in the line, pause to take pictures, personalize each signature, and generally take forever. While this was great for the image of the athlete and the company, it was a monumental pain to me and the promo team.

Of course, there were those people who stood in line, and when they finally made it to the front, pulled out a dozen balls, pucks, or jerseys and wanted them all signed. For their kids, of course. Yeah, right!

Joe Montana and me at the Atlanta Super Show. Joe was a huge draw, as people lined up all the way around our booth to get his autograph.

A couple of weeks before the Super Show in February 1993, Kelly announced he wanted to host a private dinner with Robyn Golden, the buyer from The Sports Authority. Not that there was any pressure here, but The Sports Authority was the largest retailer in the country and our biggest customer. Everybody wanted to entertain Robyn Golden, who also happened to love hanging out with famous athletes.

The heat was on me to supply a few stars for Robyn's delight, and I really came through—or so I thought. First, I secured Randall Cunningham, the All-Pro quarterback from the Philadelphia Eagles. Next, I picked up a commitment from Mark Rypien of the Washington Redskins, who had just been selected the Most Valuable Player in the Skin's drubbing of the Buffalo Bills in Super Bowl XXVII the week before. And, last but not least, David Justice of the Atlanta Braves agreed to join us. This was right after Justice had led the Braves to the 1992 World Series and was one of the hottest names in Major League Baseball.

Everything was all set, and I flew into Atlanta the day before the scheduled dinner feeling pretty good about myself. Checking into the Peachtree Plaza Hotel, I went to my room to find the red message light on the phone illuminated. It was David Justice, informing me that he had to cancel the dinner because his wife was coming in from a job, and he had to pick her up at the airport.

Damn, I thought, *he can't do that*. I needed him at the dinner, so I dialed him up. "Dave, you have to be there," I pleaded. "I told the buyer from The Sports Authority you were coming. My ass is on the line."

"OK, if it's that big of a deal I'll come," he answered, somewhat reluctantly, "but only if I can bring my wife."

Kelly had a no-wife policy at these kinds of events, but this was no time to argue. "Bring her," I said.

The next evening found us in a private room at a whoopty-doo restaurant in fashionable Buckhead. Robyn Golden and the other TSA people were sucking down cocktails and hors d'oeuvres in anticipation of meeting the big stars. Randall Cunningham was the first to show up. One down. Then Mark Rypien sauntered into the room. Two down, one to go. We waited. A half hour went by, along with a couple more cocktails, and all the while Kelly looked at me nervously.

Finally, David Justice entered the room with a woman on his arm that, to coin a phrase, a man would crawl a mile to get within an inch of. A real knockout!

With Will Clark, Dave Justice, Doug Kelly, and Jim Easton at the Easton double-decked booth at the Atlanta Super Show in February 1993.

There are some privileges accorded to those who make the arrangements, so I awarded myself one when I sat this beauty next to me. Attempting to come up with a clever line, I blurted out, "David said you just came in from a job. Tell me, Halle, what do you do?"

I had played it cool, real cool. You see, her name was Halle Berry.

Industry trade shows were not the only venues where the promo team was expected to supply star power. To motivate the sales force, we always felt it was beneficial to bring an Elway, Montana, Gossage, or Gretzky to our annual sales meetings to give a little pep talk to motivate the boys. One year we actually got permission from the National Hockey League to have the real Stanley Cup flown in for our hockey sales meeting. I swear I saw tears running down the cheeks of our Canadian Reps as they hugged the cup.

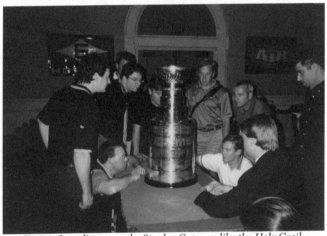

To our Canadian reps, the Stanley Cup was like the Holy Grail.

In June of 1986 our baseball/softball sales meeting was going to be held Southern California just after the Cincinnati Reds were scheduled to play the Giants in San Francisco. We had no athletes scheduled to come in for the opening speeches, so I came up with a brilliant idea. I took the company video camera up to Candlestick Park and asked Pete Rose, who was the Reds' player/manager at that time, if he would say a few words of inspiration. Pete, as always, was accommodating. Batting practice was about to start, so he was in a big hurry. We had just a couple of minutes and could only do one take.

We started rolling, and Rose was his typical self. "OK, you guys, I know you are at your meeting, so I want you to work hard. You represent Easton and Mizuno, the best brands in the game..." *Yada, yada, yada.* He was great, a real "Knute Rockne." Standing behind the camera, I was stoked, thinking how good it was going to be as an opening for the meeting.

Rose continued, "So go out and win the sales game for Easton and Mizuno, and if you ever get to Cincinnati, make sure to come to the ball park to say hello." Perfect!

But then Pete peered directly into the camera, gave a wave of his arm, winked, and signed off with, "Adios, motherf—ers!"

With that he got up and ran out the door.

I was too stunned—and disappointed—to say a word. There was no way I could have the tape edited before the meeting started, and I sure didn't think it was appropriate to show it with that final little ending. Damn!

Or was it? Before the meeting started, I showed it to Jim Easton, fully expecting him to veto the tape. After all, Masato Mizuno was going to be present, as well as some of the ladies from our office. You can imagine my surprise when Jim, hearing Rose's departing words, busted out laughing and said to let it rip.

Later the guys all wandered into the main ballroom, and when they were all seated, I walked up to the podium and announced that a special guest wanted to say a few words. The lights lowered, and Pete was up on the screen. As the tape was running, I was looking for a reaction from the men, or, should I say, non-reaction. These were professional salesmen and hearing a few words from Pete Rose on tape didn't exactly create the emotional reaction I was looking for. Until, that is, the end.

I had never seen our sales force so inspired following Pete's pep talk. It was amazing how the great orator knew exactly what to say.

Another area growing area where we needed star power is at fanfests. Fanfests at all-star games have become common, but it wasn't always so common for the National Hockey League, certainly not before 1991. Until Easton came along.

In the fall of 1990, Neil Hernberg, our hockey promo rep, and I were in New York having dinner with Fred Scalera, head of licensing for the NHL. Discussion centered on how the post-game party the NHL put on could be spiced up. I remembered seeing an ad in a hockey magazine for a plastic surface that could be laid out to simulate ice, so I blurted out, "Why don't we have a slap shot cage set up at the party so people could line up and take shots at a goalie?"

Why not, indeed. Scalera gave us the OK to work on the details, and Hernberg and I put the plan in motion. I purchased the "fake" ice and had it shipped to Chicago, the site for the all-star game. We secured netting through the Athletic Training Equipment Company, and the Chicago Black Hawks, along with fifty pucks, brought a goal to the party site. Of course, all the sticks were Easton, which we laid up in stick racks sent in from our distribution center in Salt Lake City. We even rented a set of bleachers and a popcorn machine. This was going to be authentic.

The All-Star game was played on a Saturday afternoon at the old Chicago Stadium. This was right at the beginning of the Gulf War and the place was rocking during the playing of the National Anthem.

The party was scheduled to start right after the game, and I was smug in my belief that we were all set to go with the first "reality" event at an NHL function when I realized we were missing one huge piece of the puzzle: a goalie. It wouldn't be real without one, but you don't just find a rent-a-goalie at 5:00 on a Saturday afternoon. We lucked out, though. One of the workers setting up the cage had a friend who played pick-up hockey in the city, and after an emergency call, we had our man.

The Easton shoot-out cage was a hit, and people waited in line all evening to take their shots at the goal. There were two issues, though. As the night went on, the guests were getting more and more inebriated. Watching adults in evening attire falling on their rear ends whacking at hockey pucks is pretty scary (even if it is humorous). Worse than that, though, was the fear that we were going to kill the kid in the net. I never realized how hot a goalie could get, and I'm not referring to stopping slap shots. The poor guy must have lost twenty pounds. Scalera gave him one of the All-Star game jerseys, though, and quite a few of the players came over and took some shots at him, so he was in goalie heaven by the time the evening ended.

That's how the "fanfest" originated at the NHL All-Star game.

**CHAPTER
ELEVEN**

Joys of Traveling

When I was a kid, I had a neighbor named Bob Ottesen who used to travel a lot on business. Boy, did I think that was cool! Jetting around the country and visiting all of the interesting cities and sights sounded like a terrific way to earn a living. As things turned out, it is pretty terrific. I have been able to visit all 50 states, while promoting ball bats, hockey sticks, and other Easton and Mizuno equipment.

Much to my delight, the world of sports extends beyond the borders of the United States. Trips abroad to promote the Mizuno and then the Easton brand became commonplace and led to some of my most entertaining, and embarrassing, experiences.

•••••••••••••••••••••••

Japan

In November 1979 All-Star teams representing the American League and National League flew to Japan to play a seven-game exhibition series in various stadiums on the main island of Honshu. The two squads were packed with some of the biggest names in the Major Leagues. The National League was represented by stars like Pete Rose, Dave Parker, Tug McGraw, Larry Bowa, Steve Garvey, Ted Simmons, Dave Kingman, and John Candelaria. The American League countered with the likes of Paul Molitor, Rod Carew, Bobby Murcer, Rick Burleson, Roy Smalley, Don Baylor, Ken Singleton, and Rick Dempsey. It was like taking the annual Major League All-Star game and moving it across the Pacific.

Adding to the All-Star rosters was a bevy of managers to serve as coaches, including Tommy Lasorda, Roger Craig, Bobby Winkles, and Sparky Anderson. The teams were led by the managers of the clubs that had battled in the World Series the previous month: Chuck Tanner of the victorious Pittsburgh Pirates and the Orioles' controversial Earl Weaver.

Earl Weaver and Tom Lasorda bowing to the flower girls prior to a game in Japan. Earl wasn't quite as congenial later in the series.

The television coverage for these games was expected to be huge, so Mizuno asked me to accompany the teams to ensure that as many players as possible were in their gear. I wasn't about to turn down a two-week, all-expenses paid trip to the land of the rising sun.

The Japanese fans came out in droves to see the American All-Stars. Stadiums were packed, and the television exposure was extensive across the nation. There was only one problem: The players didn't give a damn. This was nothing more than glorified exhibition games to them, and most looked upon it as a paid vacation with a wife or girlfriend.

However, Earl Weaver, who was still smarting over the Orioles bitter seven-game loss to Pittsburgh in the World Series, did give a damn. Most biting was that the Pirates had fought back from a 3-1 game deficit to take the crown. And Earl was a very competitive man.

After the first six games of the series in Japan, the teams were tied 3-3 with the rubber game to be held at the stadium in Yokohama.

As anyone who has traveled to Japan can attest, the traffic can be horrendous, which it was that day as the busses carrying the teams from the New Otani Hotel made their way to Yokohama. On one bus, Earl Weaver was simmering, slowly coming to his boiling point because he was getting an earful. Sitting in the two rows behind the Orioles' skipper were Dave Parker, John Candelaria, and Jim Bibby, all of the Pirates, joined by Pete Rose, the self-appointed voice of the National Leaguers. For two hours, in bumper-to-bumper traffic, they didn't let poor Earl forget who had won the World Series. Weaver just had to sit there and take the abuse that was heaped upon him until they finally reached the stadium.

As the representative from Mizuno, I was given credentials to roam anywhere in the stadium, so I wandered between the two locker rooms, making sure the players had all the right equipment. In the National League room, they were relaxing, playing cards, telling jokes, and enjoying themselves. They couldn't have cared less about the upcoming game. Across the hall, though, things were quite a bit different because Earl's blood was up. He called a team meeting and, to the astonishment and humor of the American Leaguers, went into a tirade. He let them know that he personally wanted them to kick the National League's ass! The more he ranted, the redder his face became—it looked like his eyes were going to pop right out of his head.

I looked around the room for the players' reactions, and noticed that almost all of them had to bite their lips to keep from laughing out loud. It looked like they were all thinking something along the lines of, "C'mon, Earl. Get serious."

Going into the third inning, the game was scoreless. With one out and a runner at first (I can't recall who), Don Baylor knocked a screaming line drive into the corner down the left field line. The runner took off on contact and scored easily, with Baylor pulling into second with an RBI double. Earl was happily clapping his hands in the dugout.

Just then, the Met's Joel Youngblood, playing second base for the National Leaguers, raised his arms and called for the ball. When it was tossed to him, he calmly walked over and stepped on second base, whereupon the Japanese umpire put his fist up in the air and called the runner out. He had missed the bag!

That's when Earl lost it. Screaming every obscenity in the English language, he bolted out of the dugout and made a beeline for the poor arbiter. In front of a packed stadium and a national television audience, Earl Weaver put on one of the greatest tirades in history. His neck veins were bulging when he went face-to-face with the Asian man in blue. Earl

Was gyrating, gesturing, kicking dirt, and calling that poor man everything in the book. Looking down the line in the American League dugout, I saw players putting towels over their heads trying to hide their laughter. A few had to walk down the tunnel and into the locker room. They didn't want to have their manager see them cracking up.

In the regular season, no umpire would have put up with such abuse and would have tossed Weaver out, but this was international diplomacy. The Japanese umpire certainly didn't want to throw Earl out of the game, so the poor guy just stood there and took it. Of course, it may have helped that he probably didn't understand a word Weaver was screaming at him.

Finally, Earl ran out of steam and tramped back to the dugout. The fans didn't know what to makes of this, so they sat in stunned silence.

Earl was not done, though; he just couldn't take it. I was no more than five feet away from him on the bench, and I saw the crescendo building. I watched the Orioles' skipper stomp his foot on the dugout floor and yell out obscenities at the top of his lungs. All of the players stared in amazement… and then laughed. Again, Earl kicked the floor and screamed out the f-word. The entire stadium could hear his rant; in fact, I wouldn't be surprised if people halfway to Tokyo heard it, too.

The home plate umpire and crew chief for the game was Bill Haller, a veteran American League arbiter who, historically, had been an adversary of Earl Weaver. At this point in the tirade, he had heard and seen just about all he could take. He flipped off his mask, pointed over to the American League dugout, and yelled, "That's enough, Earl!"

That was all Earl Weaver needed—he bolted off the bench and, the next thing I saw, he was face-to-face with

Haller, again filling the air with obscenities. Haller was not as concerned with East-West diplomacy, so Earl Weaver quickly found himself being asked to leave the premises, much to the amusement of the players.

The conclusion of the 1979 campaign was tough for Earl Weaver. Not only did his Orioles lose in seven games to the Pittsburgh Pirates in the World Series, but his American League All-Stars also lost in seven games to the National Leaguers in Japan. Losses in two hemispheres made for a bummer of a year.

Later I asked Joel Youngblood if the runner had missed the bag. He just smiled, put his hands about twelve inches apart, and said the footprint was that far from second base.

Rose, Parker, Bibby, and Candelaria made sure they were on the same bus with Earl for the two-hour trip back to the New Otani. I'll leave what was said on that ride to your imagination.

One of the more unique experiences I have enjoyed was being in Japan the night that Sadaharu Oh broke the world record for homeruns, held at that point by Hank Aaron. Of course, most Americans don't recognize Oh-san's record since all of his homeruns were hit in the Japanese professional league, but it was a big deal in Japan, and the event was splashed all over the newspapers and television stations. Without a doubt, Oh-san was a national hero.

What struck me about Oh-san was his demeanor. The man was all class as he acknowledged the cheers of the adoring fans; it didn't hurt that he played for the Tokyo Giants, the most popular team in Japan.

It was quite a thrill for me when I was able to meet Oh-san during the MLB All-Star series. Standing by the batting cage at Korakuen Stadium, the Giants' home park, I asked how he was able to hit with such power utilizing his unusual hitting style (Oh-san always lifted his front leg as the ball was being delivered, almost like a pitcher does). My thought was that off-speed pitches would throw off his timing.

Yeah, I'm going to tell Sadaharu Oh how to play the game...

He looked at me like I had just jumped off the turnip truck. Through the interpreter, he explained that he did indeed lift his lead leg and that his leg was moving forward as the pitch was being thrown. "But watch the hands," he explained, "and you will notice that they stay back until I attack the ball." He smiled and gave me a look that politely questioned whether I had ever played baseball.

Later, in reviewing tape of Oh-san batting, there it was: leg lifted and moving forward, but hands back and... *WHAM*!

Oh-san retired as a player following the 1980 season; he ended up hitting 868 homeruns in his illustrious career. It would have been interesting to see how many he would have hit in the American major leagues.

Another interesting trip to Japan involved Rickey Henderson, who was a piece of work. There simply is no better description.

Anyone who has heard interviews with the great base thief knows that Rickey had his own distinct way of dealing with the press during interviews. He regularly spoke in the third person, so no one could be sure if Rickey was referring to himself or some fictional character.

Following the 1982 season, and right after Rickey had broken Lou Brock's single-season stolen base record, the Mizuno Corporation requested that Henderson come to Japan as their guest, along with his fiancée, Pam. The plan was for Henderson to make a few appearances on behalf of the company in Tokyo, Osaka, and other key cities in Japan. For the most part, though, the trip was designed for Rickey and Pam to enjoy an all-expenses-paid, first-class trip to Japan.

I was invited to accompany the lucky couple to serve as a liaison—in other words to be the gopher who made sure everything went smoothly.

Arriving in Tokyo on a Monday, I knew from our first meeting that this was going to be a long trip. We sat with the Mizuno people to review the itinerary, which was relatively painless and easy for Rickey: an appearance every other day for one week, then a full week of sightseeing and relaxation for Rickey and Pam.

Rickey Henderson was always a showboat, even in Japan. This photo was taken while we toured the Ginza District in Tokyo. Here we are pictured with his fiancée, Pam.

That was the plan, anyway, until Pam spoke up. "There is an appearance scheduled for Rickey on Thursday, and he can't do an appearance on Thursday. It's Thanksgiving."

"In the U.S., you're right," I said, "but not here in Japan."

"It is for us, and we would like to have a full turkey dinner," Pam replied, making it clear that there would be no other options.

Trying to find a Thanksgiving dinner for two in Japan was impossible. We ended up having to fly two turkey dinners in from Seattle at a cost I'd rather forget, and the Thursday appearance was cancelled.

The next day Mizuno staged a posh press conference at the Imperial Hotel in Tokyo. All the key baseball press was in attendance since this was their first chance to hear from the great American base-stealer. Over fifty scribes and all the major television networks were on hand when Rickey entered the grand ballroom.

Rickey demonstrating his base-stealing techniques to the Tokyo Giants.

I stood off to the side while Rickey sat at the podium with the appointed interpreter, Miss Michiyo Shuto. The executive assistant to company president Masato Mizuno, Michiyo had attended Georgetown University in Washington, D.C., and spoke fluent English.

A newspaper reporter rose and asked the first question—in Japanese, of course. Michiyo turned to Rickey and eloquently translated, "He wants to know why are you so successful stealing bases."

As Henderson went through his answer, a look of bewilderment came across Shuto's face. It was obvious she could not understand a word he was saying. This was language she had never heard before—it was "Rickeynese." So, like Barbara Billingsley in *Airplane*, I stood up and offered to translate Rickeynese into English for Shuto, who then translated it into Japanese for the reporters.

Everything went smoothly after that, but it may have been the most comical press conference in Mizuno's history!

●●●●●●●●●●●●●●●●●●●●●●●●

Cuba

Since Fidel Castro came to power in 1959, Cuba has been the forbidden island in the Caribbean, at least to Americans. Luckily, through baseball, I have had the opportunity to travel there on two occasions.

The first was in October 1987 when the International Baseball Association held their annual conference in Havana. Since Easton was a sponsor of the IBA, the State Department gave me clearance to attend.

For those auto aficionados who were into 1957 Chevy's, Havana was a dream. Other than that, it was fairly dreary and oppressed. The communist way of life just didn't seem too appetizing. We were housed in what was considered a top hotel, and it was brutal: cracks in the walls, spotty plumbing, a broken air conditioner—not exactly the Waldorf-Astoria. My biggest highlight was sitting in my room and listening to the Cardinals/Giants playoff game on a radio station from the west coast of Florida. After three nights, I couldn't wait to get out of there.

On the departure day, the wind picked up, and dark clouds started gathering. When I turned on the radio, the news was that a hurricane was approaching the Florida coast, coming in right over Cuba. Oh, great!

There were only six people in the party leaving Havana for the United States, and by the time our bus reached Jose

Marti International Airport later that afternoon, the rain was
blowing sideways. The hurricane had landed. We were driven
to a small room with a thatched roof, away from the main
terminal, and told to wait. And wait. And wait. The wind
kept howling as we waited. Finally, we were put on a bus and
driven across several runways, where we pulled up in front of
a big white Boeing 727 airliner that had no markings and no
windows. This was going to be a short luxury flight courtesy
of the U.S. State Department.

The send-off from the Cuban authorities was joyful and
friendly: We left between two lines of military police holding
AK-47s at chest level. Boy, was I glad to get out of there.

The only problem was that the wind was blowing so hard
that the plane was rocking back and forth on the tarmac. As
the pilot revved the engines and we started to roll down the
runway, I thought there was no way that plane was going to
fly.

It was then that the paranoia set in. You see, one of the six
passengers was pretty famous; his name was Dr. Creighton
Hale, the President and CEO of Little League Baseball.
Everyone in the baseball world knew Dr. Hale because he had
put Little League on the world stage and had designed many
products for youth baseball, including the batting helmet. As
I sat across from Dr. Hale in this rocking, windowless tube
of aluminum, all I could think of was impending doom. The
plane was going to go down in the hurricane, and the papers
around the world the next day would say that Dr. Creighton
Hale and others perished in a plane crash somewhere over
the Caribbean, and I was going to be one of the "others."
Thankfully, it was just paranoia, and we landed safely back
on U.S. soil.

So much for my first trip to Cuba.

I must be a glutton for punishment because in 2003 I agreed to go back to Mr. Castro's island, this time as a chaperone. Chris Bradford, the baseball coach at Saint Francis High School in Mountain View, California, was taking a group of boys on a goodwill tour to Havana and a few other cities in Cuba and inquired if my wife and I wanted to go. Sarah had never been there and showed an interest, so I decided, "What the hell," and we signed on.

This was a typical baseball tour with everything arranged and itinerary set. It wasn't at all like the California All-Stars in Asia, mind you. So there really wasn't anything unusual about it, other than one moment that will forever be embedded in my mind, as well as the minds of the boys on the trip.

On our fourth day in Cuba, the entire party of kids and parents climbed aboard a beautiful, air-conditioned Mercedes bus for a five-hour ride to the city of Cienfuegos, situated on the south side of the island. Occasionally, we passed cement markers on the side of the road and, upon inquiry, were told they were monuments to the soldiers who had fallen on that spot during the ill-fated Bay of Pigs military operation in 1961. Whoops!

About forty miles outside Cienfuegos, we were driving along a one lane, pot-holed strewn highway in the middle of nowhere. All of a sudden, we came around a curve in the road, and right in front of us, in a cow pasture, there was a baseball game being played. We yelled for the driver to pull off the road.

The game was between two local town teams, with players' ages, at best estimates, everywhere from fifteen to fifty. No two players had the same uniform; there were all sorts of colors and styles, but they certainly knew who played for whom.

The field—well, it just blew us away. Our kids couldn't believe what they saw in front of them. There was no backstop and no mound, just a circle where the pitcher was supposed to throw from. Home plate, and all of the bases, were simply pieces of cloth. There was no homerun fence, just a barbwire fence in right field that separated two pastures. Both teams shared one set of catcher's gear, which amounted to one mask and a beat up chest protector but no shin guards. Between them, there was one baseball and two old aluminum ball bats. And, to top it all off, there was a horse grazing in right field.

Were there fans? You bet. It looked as though the families of all of the players were there to watch. Of course, there were no stands or bleachers, but it was a festive atmosphere with guys beating on rumba drums between innings.

I'm sure you can imagine the change in the atmosphere that happened when our Mercedes bus pulls up, and a bunch of well-to-do-kids from the U.S. popped out to watch the game. These kids all had a bag on the bus with their own $300 bat, $150 glove, $100 pair of spikes, and… Well, you get the picture.

The game was briefly halted, and the Cuban players all came over to meet the Americans. One of the chaperones on the trip was Carney Lansford, the former American League All-Star third baseman, so the Cubans were fired up to meet and talk to him, and the atmosphere once again became festive.

After a while, with the translators going back and forth, it was agreed that our boys would play in the game with the Cuban players (a picture from that game is featured on the cover of this book). The Americans were divided up, and it was time to play ball—and have the experience of a lifetime.

Here I'm holding one of the two bats the teams from Cuba had to play their games. Think that bat had been used much? Don't let the condition of the field and the uniforms fool you—these guys could play and really had a passion for the game. They taught our young players a thing or two.

If only diplomacy could be handled like that.

It was finally time to move on, though, as we had a schedule to keep. After a lot of hugs and handshakes, we boarded our air-conditioned Mercedes bus, but not before two poignant things happened, which left impressions that none of us would soon forget. First, Coach Bradford hopped into the bus and came out with two boxes of brand-new Rawlings baseballs, one for each team. Many of the Cuban players broke down and cried, they were so thankful for the balls. Second, as we drove off, the two teams boarded their transportation back to their respective towns: carts drawn by horses. They all waved and smiled, without a care in the world.

Because I know you were curious, yes, the two old aluminum bats were Easton bats.

•••••••••••••••••••••••••

Europe

The largest sporting goods show in Europe, ISPO, was held every year in Munich, Germany, and that is where I was headed in September 1988. It was a tough assignment, but someone had to do it.

I was telling Joe Safety of the Financial News Network about my assignment over the phone when he tossed out an idea. FNN planned to televise the final game of the upcoming World Baseball Championship Tournament from Parma, Italy. Since I was already planning to be in Europe, and since my pal Byron Day was going to handle the play-by-play, he asked if I'd consider joining the broadcast team as color commentator. My response was automatic: "Hell, yes! Where do I sign up?"

It just so happened that the World Baseball Championships were scheduled to take place just prior to the Seoul Olympics where, for the first time, baseball would be a medal sport. However, Cuba, which dominated the amateur game, was boycotting the Olympics, so, in reality, the event in Italy was going to be the real "championship."

What a battle it would be. The Cuban team was always major league quality, particularly since Fidel Castro didn't allow his star players to leave the island to play professionally in the United States. Guys like second baseman Antonio Pacheco, third baseman Omar Linares, and centerfielder Victor Cruz had dominated the amateur baseball world for years. They were major league stars wrapped in the hypocrisy of amateur status.

Team USA, on the other hand, was entirely made up of amateur players, many of whom went on to have tremendous success in the major leagues. The pitching staff included Jim Abbott, Joe Slusarsky, Andy Benes, Ben McDonald, and Charlie Nagy. In the field, Team USA produced such future MLB stars as Ed Sprague, Tino Martinez, Robin Ventura, Tom Goodwin, and Scott Servais.

All signs pointed to a classic showdown and an intriguing broadcast if these two bitter rivals could advance to the championship game. Luckily for us, that is exactly what happened. Both Team Cuba and Team USA swept through the preliminary rounds, and the showdown was set to be played in Parma, Italy.

Concluding my four days at ISPO, which included a couple of duty calls on the famed Hofbräuhaus, I flew to Milan and hooked up with Byron. From there we hopped on a train for the two-hour ride to Parma. We spent the time going over the *dos* and *don't*s of broadcasting a ballgame, as I was new to the gig. Arriving in Parma, we picked up our credentials and started pouring over the stats from all of the previously played games. I was really going to be prepared for this.

The game was going to be broadcast live throughout Italy and back to Cuba, with their own broadcasters. Ours was to be sent back to the United States and seen on tape delay the next day. To be clear, this was not exactly the highest quality broadcast. The Italian production team only included three cameras, and coordination from the production truck parked at the stadium was spotty at best.

It was not too surprising, then, that just as we started the broadcast all I could hear was Spanish coming through my headphones. A producer in the truck had crossed some wires. For the first three innings of the game, I heard the Cuban broadcast team pounding in my head.

Instant replays were also quite a challenge. No producer in the truck spoke English, and when they wanted to show a replay, they just ran it with no warning to Byron or me. We would be right in the middle of explaining a play and *poof!* On the screen was action that had nothing to do with what we were attempting to describe for the audience. Talk about improvising! I don't think Howard Cosell or John Madden ever went through anything like that.

As tough as it was to broadcast, though, the game was turning out to be a classic. The Cubans started Rene Arocha, who later was the first player from the island to defect to the United States and play in the major leagues. Team USA countered with All-American Jim Abbott from the University of Michigan. Handicapped by not having a right hand, Abbott nonetheless went on to have a stellar career pitching for the California Angels and New York Yankees.

Arocha and Abbott matched pitch for pitch until the fourth inning when Tino Martinez swatted a hanging slider over the right field wall to give Team USA a 2-1 lead. It stayed that way going into the bottom of the ninth inning. Abbott was three outs away from shutting down the mighty Cubans.

That's when all hell broke loose.

The Cuban leadoff hitter smacked a two-hopper to Robin Ventura, who briefly bobbled the ball. Recovering, Ventura gunned his throw to Martinez, the ball easily beating the Cuban runner to the bag. One out—the first, most important out. Except the Italian umpire put his palms down in the "safe" sign. Safe? We couldn't believe it because that play hadn't even been a close one. Forgetting I was on a live microphone, I screamed out, "Bullshit!" only to then feel the sting of Byron's backhand across my skull. Whoops!

Stanford's Mark Marquess, head coach of Team USA, bolted out of the dugout to protest the call, joining Martinez, Abbott, and half of the U.S. team, but the umpire didn't budge. There was no way he could have called that runner safe, yet he did. The Cubans didn't let that gift go to waste. They quickly pushed two runs across the plate to take the World Championship, leading to a bitter defeat for Team USA.

Even though the tournament was over, Byron and I still had a job to do. FNN planned to show the championship game via tape delay, so we had to send the footage back to the U.S. Sounds archaic today, but that is what we set out to do early the next morning. We hopped a train to Milan, and two hours later transferred to a bus headed to the International Airport. Then we headed over to the Federal Express office to overnight the tape to New York because it absolutely, positively had to be there the next day. However, unknown to Byron and me, this particular day happened to be a national holiday in Italy, so Fed Ex (and any other shipping company, for that matter) wasn't open for business. The tape had to be in New York so it could be aired the next evening, but it was stuck in Italy with us. We were screwed!

We quickly reformulated our plan. Byron and I bolted for the International terminal and looked at the monitor to see what flights were leaving for New York. An Alitalia plane was scheduled to depart in a couple of hours, which was good for us. We stood by the ticket counter, looking for a candidate. Then we saw her: an American-looking young lady. I carefully approached her and said, "Excuse me, miss, I know this may sound crazy, but…" I explained our plight to her, trying my hardest not to look like some fanatical terrorist. At first, she was very reluctant, but Byron and I did our best smooth talking, and we finally convinced her that we were for real. Of course, I promised to send her a free softball bat if she completed the delivery.

Ten hours later, for the price of one Easton softball bat, the hesitant young lady delivered the tape of the championship game to an FNN staffer as she came out of customs at John F. Kennedy Airport. Later that night, fans across the country were able to tune into one heck of a ball game.

Nobody said it was going to be easy.

•••••••••••••••••••••••••

Australia

Like most Americans, I always had a tremendous urge to see Australia. What is it about the land-down-under that we love so much?

Baseball was growing in popularity across Australia in the late 1980s, and by 1990 there was a very competitive "pro" league up and running. The "pro" status came from the fact that the players were given a small stipend to play, and the league was able to negotiate a contract to have some games aired by one of the national television networks. In addition, each of the teams had a working agreement with major league clubs in the U.S. to carry a couple of minor league players. Since the season in Australia was reversed from that in the States, this gave some of the lucky chosen players an extra chance to hone their skills without having to go play in Mexico, Puerto Rico, Venezuela, or the Dominican Republic. English was the main language, and the beaches were terrific. Plus, everyone knew the Aussies were wild and crazy (in a good way), which gave Easton some great reasons to sign a supplier agreement with the Australian Baseball

League (ABL) to be the "official bat," which in turn gave me a great excuse to fly to Melbourne in October of 1991.

At this time Easton was not an unknown name in Australia. Through a newly established office, the company had been attempting to sell Easton-branded field hockey sticks and a variety of products for the sport of cricket, including bats and gloves. Swan Richards, a charismatic cricket aficionado, headed up the sales and marketing of these products. In one of his more notorious moves, Swan signed an endorsement agreement with the Victorian Cricket Association for quite a bit of money.

Truth be told, we never sold a large amount of cricket bats, but the perks were impressive, such as tickets to the exclusive VCA box for the Aussie Rules Football semi-final championship game at the famed Melbourne Cricket Grounds. This was a gorgeous, circular stadium that held nearly 80,000 screaming fans. Australians are as fanatical about their brand of football as Americans are about the gridiron.

Being invited to enjoy the big match in the Victorian Cricket Association box was no small deal; it was a first-class event. Coats and ties were required for the men, dresses for the ladies. Everything was prim and proper.

Since I knew nothing about Aussie Rules Football, I asked Swan to give me the lowdown on who was the most famous player on the field that day. "Gary Abblett, mate. He plays for Geelong, and he's the one to watch."

I was perplexed when I reviewed the game program and found that Abblett, while certainly being a star player, had missed a season. I asked Swan why. "Well, you see, he came home from a match one night and found his wife in the rack with the pizza delivery bloke. Abblett knocked him around a bit and had to spend some time in the pen." Now, I never found out if Swan was telling me the truth, but his story sure opened my eyes to the world of Aussie Rules.

The game was terrific—fast and hard-hitting with no interruptions, like huddles, between plays. The best part, though, are the fans, who are rowdy as hell. To put it mildly, Aussie Rules Football is a very entertaining sport.

I left quite an impression on my Australian hosts, too. During the game, Ken Jacobs, the Executive Director of the VCA, politely introduced me to all of his guests in the box. One elderly lady, roughly in her eighties, was extremely kind. She wanted to know what had brought me to the land-down-under and inquired about our business, my hometown, my family—you name it. She was really classy and going out of her way to make me feel welcome.

Not to be outdone I wanted to show interest in her, as well. So, in a voice that could be heard by people all around the box, I asked, "Which of these two teams do you root for?" Gasp! Horror! The box went silent, and all eyes turned on me. The nice old lady turned beet red, and I thought she was going to faint. For little did I know that, in Australia, the term "to root" has a far different meaning than it does in the United States.

So much for the ugly American.

●●●●●●●●●●●●●●●●●●●●●●●●●

Air travel

While I love traveling, I have found that air travel is not always as much fun or as exciting as it is cracked up to be. The constant waiting, standing in line, and hours spent on the planes are taxing, to say the least. Like all business travelers,

I have had experiences that, at the time, were extremely frustrating but became laughable as time went on. I've had three that still make me shake my head—sometimes both in frustration and laughter.

The first was back in 1979. I was on a Delta commuter travelling from Cincinnati to Columbus, Ohio, to attend a major softball tournament. Though it was a small commuter plane, I was surprised to see that I was the only passenger. It was just me, the flight attendant, and the two pilots—sort of like my own personal aircraft. How cool was that? Cool, that is, until we arrived in Columbus, and my luggage did not. How in the world could an airline lose a bag when there's only one passenger? The station manager got an earful for that one.

My second bizarre experience occurred in November 1990. Concluding a marketing meeting in Memphis, I rushed to catch the Northwest Airlines flight back home to San Francisco. Boarding the flight, I glanced into the cockpit and, lo and behold, there sat my brother-in-law, John Hendricks—Captain John was steering the ship. After a quick exchange of *hello*s, I sauntered down the aisle to my seat at the back of the bus (first class is not normally in the cards for members of the sporting goods business).

About an hour into the flight I was feeling parched and in need of an adult beverage. Due to the fact that the company frowned on paying for drinks, on the ground or up in the air, I thought I could tap into my connection in the cockpit. I drafted a note and hit the overhead button to hail the flight attendant. Handing her the piece of paper, I asked if she would take it up to the pilot. It did not dawn on me, until I saw the horrid look on her face, that perhaps that wasn't such a good idea. I don't think I fit the profile of a terrorist, but

it was a naïve move, nonetheless. She was finally convinced
that the story about my brother-in law was legit and took the
note, though I never did get a drink.

The adventure did not end there, however. As we
approached San Francisco, I noticed that we were flying
around in circles; fog had blown in and covered the air
field. So we circled... and circled. After what seemed like an
eternity of circling, Captain John came over the intercom and
announced he was sorry, but due to low ceilings, the flight
was diverting to Los Angeles. That isn't necessarily unusual,
especially for San Francisco, but when it happens to you, it is
rather irritating. Acts of nature are a small consolation for a
major inconvenience!

Landing in Los Angeles, we were told that the airline
would provide transportation to a hotel, but before we could
go to any hotel, we were all stuck standing in a long line at
the customer service desk in order to book our flights out
the next morning, which, as you might guess, was not exactly
fun. To be sociable, I waited for the crew to exit the plane,
figuring Captain John and I could grab a beer or two since
we were both stranded for the night. That's when I got my
first lesson about the FAA and the Boeing 757 aircraft. My
brother-in-law informed me that he was just getting off the
plane to use the restroom and grab a quick snack because he
was going to immediately take off and fly the plane to... San
Francisco. What? As he explained it to me, the 757 was so
technologically advanced that it could literally fly itself, fog
or no fog. He was going to fly on but without me and the rest
of the passengers. While I slept in a flea-bag hotel somewhere
on Century Boulevard, Captain John got to sleep in his own
bed in the comfort of his own home. Oh, and by the way, the
flight attendant never did give him my note.

The third experience, while I can chuckle today, almost had me beyond restraint at the time.

In August 2010, I was in Spokane, Washington, handling the play-by-play over the web at the American Legion World Series. The morning after the championship game, I was scheduled to fly to Williamsport, Pennsylvania, for a meeting at the Little League World Series. The route called for flights from Spokane to Seattle, Seattle to Philadelphia, and a final leg on a USAir commuter into Williamsport. I had arranged the meeting, which included, among others, Steve Keener, the President/CEO of Little League International, and Chris Zimmerman, the new CEO of Easton Sports. Failure to show up at such a meeting was not an option!

As I mentioned earlier, in most cases, I sit in the back of the plane. Every once in a while, due to miles accumulated, I get bumped up to first class. It's rare but always appreciated, particularly on coast-to-coast flights. When the lady at the ticket counter in Spokane handed me the boarding passes with the Seattle to Philadelphia segment showing seat 3A (*First class!*), I was more than pleased.

Landing in Seattle, I had an hour to kill, so I went over to the nearest Starbucks for some coffee. There was no need for me to eat, as meals in first class were always pretty tasty and filling.

Finally, the call for boarding the first class section was made, and I stepped up and handed my boarding pass to the gate agent. When he put it through the scanner, nothing happened. He tried again, but again nothing happened. He told me I had to speak to the representative at the service desk and asked me to step out of line so other passengers could board. I was now a bit hot under the collar, but there was no use in arguing with him.

Watching the passengers board the flight, I waited in the service desk line, finally making my way to the front. Explaining my plight to the USAir representative, she casually looked into the computer screen and told me that they had no record of me in their system. I tried to laugh. No record in their system? Then how in the world could I have a boarding pass to Philadelphia and one to Williamsport? Even more than that, how did I fly from Spokane to Seattle if I wasn't in their system? It had to be a joke.

What wasn't a joke, though, was that the boarding process had now been completed, and they were getting ready to shut the door. While I was concerned, the USAir rep didn't show any emotion at all. She stated that since she could not find any record of me, there was nothing she could do to help me. Nada. She didn't have a clue how I could have boarding passes for all of my connecting flights, and she really didn't care. I asked her who was sitting in seat 3A, so she checked the monitor and stated the seat was empty. My seat!

When I glanced over to the gate again, the door was being shut and the plane started backing away. That's when I lost it and demanded that I be able to speak with a manager. Finally, after being warned to calm down, a USAir rep in authority heard me out. Like his compatriot, while he didn't understand how this could have happened, there was nothing he could do to help. After all, the flight had departed. Oh, and by the way, all seats heading to the East coast were sold out for the rest of the day. It was like a scene out of *Candid Camera*, or worse, out of the *Twilight Zone*.

Finally, they came up with one solution. There was one middle seat in the back of the plane on a flight to Charlotte. From there I could sit for two hours and catch a flight to Newark, New Jersey, which would arrive at midnight. To complete the Odyssey, I could then rent a car and drive the four hours to Williamsport. I had thirty minutes to run to the gate for the Charlotte flight, while trying to get in touch with Hertz to reserve the rental car in Newark.

By the time I settled in my seat on the plane, sweating and out of breath, in seat 29E (and everyone knows what an E seat means), I realized I was famished. Looking forward to that first-class fare on the Philadelphia flight, I had not dined when I had the chance to in Seattle. Not to worry, though. The flight attendant announced there were sandwiches for sale on board, and they would soon be coming down the aisle, and the turkey wrap they described sounded scrumptious.

You may be able to guess the rest of the story. When the meal cart arrived at row 28, they ran out of food. Sorry, sir! There was nothing until the plane arrived in Charlotte.

The long (there is no short to this) journey continued on to Newark, where I grabbed the rental car and drove on to Williamsport, arriving at 5:30 in the morning—just in time to grab a cat nap and shower before the scheduled 9:00 a.m. meeting.

Somewhere, in cyberspace, is the answer to how I could have a boarding pass for a flight when nobody at the airline even knew I existed, but I'll probably never know.

Ah, the joys of travel.

●●●●●●●●●●●●●●●●●●●●●●●●●

Fate has a strange way of dictating if any of us are in the "right" place or "wrong" place at any given time.

On Sunday, September 9, 2001, Dan Mecrones, Easton's top hockey promotions man, called me up. "Darbs, do I have to be at the meeting on Tuesday? I'm in the middle of training camps, and it would be better use of my time calling on the teams now than coming out to Los Angeles," he explained.

It was the practice at Easton to hold three marketing/ strategy meetings each year, and one was scheduled for that Tuesday, September 11.

I always wanted Danny to be at these meetings. As a former college and minor league hockey player, he was much more knowledgeable than me, and I could always count on him to be a voice of reason representing the promo team. But in this case, he had a good argument. The NHL camps were in full swing, and two or three days lost coming out to meetings in California could lose us players to competitors. After mulling it over in my mind for a few seconds, I told him to bag it, and I would cover for him at the meeting.

Two days later, at 6:00 a.m., the Southwest Airlines plane I was on, supposedly heading to Burbank Airport (and the strategy meeting), was at the end of the runway, waiting to take off. All of a sudden the pilot came on the intercom to announce that we were returning to the gate but offered no explanation. I sat in my seat thinking, "Why the delay? Mechanical problems? Damn Southwest."

As I was walking up the jetway with all of the other disgruntled passengers, my cell phone rang. On the line was Dan Jelinek, our VP/Sales. "Darbs, where's Mecrones?"

"Why?" I wondered. I was pretty sure I'd told Jelinek that Danny wasn't coming to the meeting.

By this time, I was in the terminal and saw the view on the television monitors of the burning Twin Towers.

"Wasn't Mecrones flying out here this morning?" Jelinek frantically asked again.

Fate, indeed, intervened in the case of Dan Mecrones. Had it not been for his insistence to call on the NHL teams

in training camp, he would have been on American Airlines
Flight 11, the first plane to hit the Twin Towers.

You just never know.

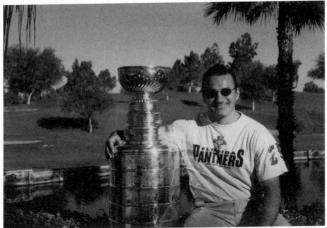

Dan Mecrones with the Stanley Cup. Fate, along with the desire to call on his NHL teams, saved his life on 9/11.

CHAPTER
TWELVE

The Good

Negotiating endorsement contracts with professional athletes, coaches, and teams is a key part of the job description for many promotion people in the sporting goods business. While it can, at times, be both exciting and challenging, it also can be tedious and frustrating. In a way, it's like gambling. You bet on the entity you are signing and investing in, hoping they will give the company a valuable return by creating the demand that pushes the products onto the dealers' shelves (the "push-in") and then sells them off to consumers (the "sell-through"). The good signings are those that create exposure for the brand that is more than anticipated—where the athlete performs at a level far above the value of the contract.

In recent years there have been athletes who have transcended all markets. These are individuals who are known worldwide and have not only performed at the highest level but also have personalities to match their athletic accomplishments. The most obvious names in this category include Tiger Woods and Michael Jordan. Whatever they pitched turned to gold, which resulted in tons of sales for their sponsors.

Finding a Tiger Woods or Michael Jordan is like finding a needle in a haystack. Usually, when signing an athlete, you look for a league MVP or, if signing a team, national championship quality; in other words, you want entities with high television exposure.

Over the past twenty years, the endorsement negotiation game has changed. In the late seventies and through the eighties, in my early years at Curley-Bates and Easton Sports, negotiations were normally between the athlete and me. It was rare, indeed, to have an agent involved. Getting to the athletes was simple. If one was part of the industry and conducted himself professionally, there was access to the locker room. Promotion people were generally accepted by the athletes, and long-term friendships were established whether or not the athletes used the products.

That friendly environment started to undergo a change in 1985 after the cocaine scandals developed in Major League Baseball. Commissioner Ueberroth ordered the clubs to tighten security, which meant it was harder to gain access to the locker rooms. That access has become even tougher with the steroid scandals.

The biggest impact on the relationship between the promotion people and the athletes, though, has been the increasing role that agents play in the lives of their clients. Agents now want to control everything their players are involved with; in other words, they want a piece of the action, which can amount to twenty percent of the endorsement deal.

Over the years, I have developed one rule: Do not sign a player to a rich endorsement deal for "known" products.

Unless there is some shock value to the deal, it generally isn't worth entering into it. For example, the contract Easton signed with Will "The Thrill" Clark in 1990 had no shock value; this story is not a knock on the Thrill, who was a terrific ballplayer. However, Clark was already established, and we were looking for him to garner exposure for products (ball gloves, batters gloves) that were already in the market place. There was nothing new about these kinds of products, and it was a very expensive contract, yet it did not create the demand that Easton had banked on.

This picture was taken at the press conference the day we announced the signing of Will Clark. Doug Kelly is in front with Will "The Thrill" while I'm in the back, flanked by Jim Easton and Will's agent, Jeff Moorad.

Conversely, the contract Easton signed with Wayne Gretzky was extremely valuable because Gretzky, in signing with Easton, was switching from a traditional wooden stick to an aluminum stick, which was revolutionary and gave immediate credibility to metal sticks.

Mizuno's signing of Pete Rose in 1979 had the same effect, not because Pete was going to use new, revolutionary products, but because he was going to endorse a new name in the market place—and a foreign brand, to boot. The effect of his signing was immediate and had a great impact.

For over thirty years I have gone through the pleasures, disappointments, hassles, joys, and challenges of signing hundreds of professional athletes to use and endorse Easton and Mizuno products from hockey sticks to football pads to ball gloves. There are stories that, looking back now, I might say I just got lucky, and my gambling paid off. Some of those stories involve signing players who were unknown at the time but who became well-known later on; other stories involve using our products wisely; and still others involve high-profile athletes who knew how to help us sell the name.

●●●●●●●●●●●●●●●●●●●●●●●●

Gambling on an unknown player

In the spring of 1978, during the first camp tour of the Mizuno Baseball Workshop, the goal was to sign up "known" Major Leaguers, which was easier said than done, because almost all the players on the forty-man rosters were already taken by established brands, such as Rawlings and Wilson. We called on the Dodgers at Vero Beach, and a lot of players came into the Workshop, more out of curiosity than for any other reason. We gave ball gloves to just about anyone who would take them: Steve Garvey, Reggie Smith, Joe Ferguson, and Davey Lopes, just to name a few. It was great that we got our gloves in their hands, but they were already hooked up with other manufacturers. I was looking for someone, anyone, to sign on when a young man, sporting a huge afro, stepped into the Workshop and started picking through some of the gloves. He was very polite and soft-spoken. Better yet, he mentioned that he had no agreement with another glove company and was willing to sign with us for a couple of gloves each year. Desperate, I pulled out a contract without doing any fact-finding, and we both inked it on the spot. I looked at the name: Dave Stewart.

As soon as he exited the Workshop, I pulled out the Dodgers media guide to check out how good my signee was. It didn't look great; the year before, Stew, a non-roster invitee, had recorded a 4-10 record with an astronomical ERA at the Double-A level. My spirits sank pretty quickly.

However, Stew eventually made it to the Big Leagues with the Dodgers in 1981, pitching with moderate success in a relief role until being traded to the Texas Rangers during the 1983 season. The 1984 and 1985 seasons were disastrous, and Stew found himself in Philadelphia for the start of the 1986 campaign. After eight appearances and a 6.57 ERA, he was released by the Phillies. It was the end of the road.

End of the road, that is, until he received a call from Tony La Russa, the new manager of the Oakland A's, a club desperate for arms.

During the next four years, Dave Stewart won eighty-four games—the only pitcher in the Big Leagues to win at least twenty games in each season. He also captured Most Valuable Player honors in the A's World Series victory over the cross-town rival San Francisco Giants. Signing Dave Stewart that day in 1978 suddenly didn't look so bad...

This poster with Dave Stewart had the caption What Dave Stewart wears on game days *across the top.*

This photo was taken the day of the shoot for the poster above; in the group shot are Bob Sproul and John McDaniel from our ad agency. (Female make-up artist unknown.)

That same fateful day in 1978, just before we closed up, Nobe Kawano, the Dodgers Equipment Manager, brought a young player into the Workshop. He explained the youngster did not have a ball glove contract and was, in his opinion, a pretty good prospect. The young man was just a year removed from pitching in the College World Series for Eastern Michigan University, and his name was Bob Welch.

Feeling I owed it to Nobe for trying to help us, I signed a deal with Welch, not expecting much from him that year. After all, he was slated to go to Double-A to start the season.

He did go back to Double-A—until he was called up in August and helped lead the Dodgers into the 1978 World Series against the Yankees. Few will forget the showdown between Welch and slugger Reggie Jackson, as Mr. October struck out with two down in the ninth inning to seal the Dodger victory in game two of the Fall Classic.

That was very good prospecting in Vero Beach!

At another stop in March of 1978, a tall, gangly guy came through the door of the Baseball Workshop, looking to pick out a ball glove. Sporting a high number on the back of his Oriole uniform, it was obvious he was a non-roster invitee; in other words, he was a player not likely to open the season in Baltimore. His name was Ed Farmer.

In our first spring of operation, I was not in a position to turn down many players that showed an interest in the Mizuno gloves, so Farmer was certainly successful in obtaining what he came in for. Sure enough, Farmer was a victim of too many quality pitchers on the Orioles and ended up being released at the end of spring training.

That was the last I heard of, or from, Farmer until the end of December, ten months later. I was at my in-laws in Newport Beach and stupidly checked my voice messages.

There was one from Farmer, imploring an immediate return call; *immediate* carries a sense of panic for me, so I dialed him right back.

Ed Farmer discusses gloves with Yoshi Tsubota, Mizuno's top glove craftsman, and me in the Workshop.

"I'm leaving for winter ball in Puerto Rico, and I've lost my glove. I need another one right now," he explained. He also told me he had signed on with the Brewers after being released by Baltimore and had spent the season in Triple-A.

"No problem. I'll send one out tomorrow," I told him, thinking that was pretty good service.

That wasn't good enough. "I'm leaving tonight. I need the glove today," he replied. All I needed to do was procure a glove for him during the Christmas holidays.

As every sales/promo rep should, I always had samples in the trunk of my car, and luckily it turned out that he was calling from Santa Monica, only an hour's drive from Newport. Nixing a fabulous dinner, I left the table and a furious wife to drive up the 405 to deliver the glove to Farmer. Santa himself couldn't have done a better job.

Farmer ended up signing with the Texas Rangers in 1979 and made the ball club coming out of spring training. The Rangers then traded him to the White Sox, where he flourished for three seasons, racking up fifty-four saves for the South-Siders and being selected to the 1980 American League All-Star team.

Farmer was a strange duck, and I had my issues with him later down the road; however, for those three seasons, he used the Mizuno ball glove because I played Santa during the Christmas season.

When I called on the Oakland Athletics in 1980, which was the first year Mizuno footwear was promoted at the Major League level, Rickey Henderson was a young rookie. One of the benefits in having the A's as my "home" team was that they were, at that time, a terrible ball club. Charlie Finley had just sold the team to the Haas family, though, and Billy Martin had taken over as manager, so the future was looking brighter. There were positive signs from the players' side, too. With Mike Norris, Matt Keough, Rick Langford, Steve McCatty, and Brian Kingman, the young pitching staff was comprised of arms that would make up one of the American League's top rotations a year later, and there was some potent lumber in the line-up with Tony Armas, Dwayne Murphy, and Wayne Gross.

The budding star, though, was the young kid from Oakland Technical High School, Rickey Henderson. I am sure that if Rickey had been on more high profile teams we never would have had the chance to sign him. Being in Oakland, though, he was flying under the radar, so he signed and two seasons later stole 130 bases to break Lou Brock's Major League record for a single season. Mizuno shoes became synonymous with the great base thief—and there is no better story to sell or promote baseball shoes.

You could say Rickey was a steal—for Mizuno. That didn't mean we didn't have to work to keep him, though.

Rickey Henderson was never short of surprises. One time we flew him down to Anaheim to make an appearance at the National Sporting Goods Association show at the Convention Center. As always, he was outgoing and engaging with our customers; Rickey could really turn on the charm when it suited him.

After the show, George Sheldon treated us all to a very expensive and elegant dinner in Newport Beach. As with any dinner hosted by Sheldon, the wine flowed freely. I ended up driving the group back to the hotel in Anaheim with Rickey sitting in the backseat, right in my sight in the rear view mirror. Occasionally, I noticed him putting something up to his mouth, giving the impression that he was simply spitting tobacco juice, as was common with ball players. I didn't give it a second thought.

Arriving back at the hotel, Sheldon took the keys to the rental car since he was planning to get up at the crack of dawn in order to catch a flight back to the Bay Area so he could watch his beloved Stanford take the gridiron against USC that afternoon. That was a bad move because at 6:00 a.m., George opened the door to the rental car and almost passed out from the stench. It turns out it wasn't tobacco juice Rickey was spitting into the bottle on the drive back from dinner. Instead, it was his way of giving the wine he had consumed back to the community, and it was most generous of him to leave the bottle, with its sordid contents, in the backseat.

If all of this insinuates that Rickey Henderson was aloof or unintelligent, he was far from it. He was the most street-smart athlete I ever dealt with and a very shrewd negotiator in an era when most athletes handled their own endorsement agreements.

The initial deal we signed with Henderson expired at the end of 1983. Being one of our "name" athletes, we certainly wanted to extend the contract. The marketing managers had packaging and ad concepts ready to go and were just waiting for me to get Rickey signed to implement the plans.

We met, and, during lunch, I committed the cardinal sin of negotiation. Over and over, I kept telling Rickey how great he was and how our marketing plans all centered on him. He kept nodding, taking it all in. Finally, I stated our offer, and he responded, "Draft it up for me and let's meet next week."

Elated, I floated back to the office, announcing to all that the deal was done, and they could proceed with all of their plans. I was really proud of myself.

I was proud, that is, until I met Rickey the following week with the contract in tow for him to sign. When I handed it to Henderson, he glanced at it and said, "I think this looks OK, but in thinking about it, there are a few small changes I want to make." One of those changes involved doubling the initial offer.

This little escapade went on three more times, and, on each occasion, the ante went up. By this time, though, our marketing team had sunk so much capital into the Henderson ads, packaging, and poster concepts that we had no choice but to pay the higher dollars. Rickey knew exactly what he was doing and played me for the fool. He taught me a valuable, albeit expensive, lesson on the art of negotiating.

Another athlete I signed on in 1983, using my recently honed negotiating skills, was Mike Scott. A terrific pitcher during his collegiate career at Pepperdine University, Scott was a top draft pick of the New York Mets. However, after his Big League debut in 1979, Scott's career in New York was mediocre, at best. In four years with the Mets he was 14-27, so companies were not exactly beating down his door to sign him to an endorsement deal. Except us—we were looking for bodies.

In 1983, though, two events changed Scott's fortunes. First, he was traded to the Houston Astros. Second, and more significant, he learned how to throw the split-fingered fastball. Over the next seven seasons, Scott was arguably the most dominating pitcher in the major leagues and was constantly pictured, along with his Mizuno products, in all of the national sports publications, including *Sports Illustrated*. In 1986, he accomplished the feat that is a dream of every pitcher: throwing a no-hitter on the final day of the season to clinch the pennant for his ball club.

It didn't hurt our cause, either, that the headquarters for Oshman's, the largest sporting goods retailer in the country at that time, was in Houston.

In the world of football, the first 49er to wear Mizuno football shoes was offensive tackle Bubba Paris. This alone did not put him into my personal hall of fame, but he also turned another Niner on to our brand. Prior to the opening of training camp, Bubba suggested I talk to fullback Roger Craig, who was about to enter his second NFL campaign.

Exciting? Not really, because Craig was virtually unknown outside the Bay Area. Though he was a starter at the University of Nebraska, he spent much of his time blocking for Heisman Trophy winner Mike Rozier. As a rookie with San Francisco, he took a backseat to running back Wendell Tyler. Since football was new to our product line, we still needed names, so we hooked up with Roger. And thrived. That same year Craig became the first player to score three touchdowns in a

Super Bowl as the 49ers destroyed the Miami Dolphins. The following year, Roger became the first NFL player to rush for over one thousand yards and have over one thousand receiving yards in the same season. His photo, including his Mizuno-clad feet, was all over the newspapers and sports magazines.

Thanks, Bubba!

•••••••••••••••••••••••••
Strategic use of products

In the early nineties, Easton began marketing and distributing the Donzis brand of football pads; of course, it was difficult to garner much exposure for protective padding since it is worn under the uniform.

Mark Dupes, our promotion manager for football products, came up with a unique idea. His plan was to sign up NFL players that were known for their toughness and reputations for being "big hitters" on the field. The deal was that the player would use our pads and also grant Easton the rights to use his name as part of the Easton/Donzis All-Hit team. In return, Easton agreed to donate free pads to the player's former high school team. It was a win-win for both parties.

Dupes did a great job selling the program to NFL stars, signing up big name players such as Reggie White, Joey Fulcher, Billy Bates, Joey Browner, Steve Atwater, Billy Ray Smith, and Andre Tippet.

Of those, it was Atwater who gave Easton the biggest bang. The Broncos' strong safety was one of the fiercest hitters in the game. One evening, in front of a Monday Night Football audience, he put a lick on Christian Okouye, the Kansas City

Chief's fullback, that many regard as the best in NFL history. The two met head-on at the line of scrimmage, and Okouye was knocked back about ten yards. It was a highlight reel play.

The following week, again on Monday Night Football, the Atwater hit was the topic of the halftime show. Dan Dierdorf, the announcer, ran the play over and over while holding up a sample of the pads Atwater wore, which we happily supplied for the set. It was fantastic exposure for a product that was usually hidden from view.

Dupes' idea was certainly a hit!

We also strategically used wristbands, which are certainly not a product that produces large revenues. However, on the appropriate wrists, they can give valuable exposure to a brand, particularly when those wrists belong to a Super Bowl quarterback.

Early in the 1992 season I received a call from Mark Rypien, QB for the Washington Redskins because he was looking to buy some hockey sticks for his brother. I told him that could be arranged and, as an afterthought, asked if he would he consider wearing the Easton wristbands. The price of those hockey sticks would certainly go down, if he knew what I meant.

A couple of months later, Rypien led the Skins to a Super Bowl victory over the Buffalo Bills, gathering MVP honors along the way. And, best of all, there was a shot on the cover of *Sports Illustrated* of Rypien with Easton wristbands.

In 1984, we had a new line of Curley-Bates football glove that went by the brand name of OLLO, which was Sheldon's brainchild. As he saw it, no matter which way you looked at the letters, it still read *OLLO*. It made sense, I guess. Randy White, a Hall of Fame defensive end who was known as one of the greatest players to ever put on the uniform of the

Dallas Cowboys, signed an endorsement deal to use Mizuno football shoes and the new OLLO gloves in the summer of 1984.

The Curley-Bates marketing managers wanted to shoot an ad using Randy and Rickey Henderson sporting the OLLO gloves, which would cover two sports with one ad, using two of the biggest names for both. By this time Henderson was a member of the New York Yankees, and the Bronx Bombers schedule had them coming to Oakland for a three-game series with the A's over Memorial Day weekend. Getting Rickey to the shoot was easy—he had to be there. The trick was getting Randy White to take the time on a national holiday to fly half-way across the country.

While Randy White may show a mean demeanor on the gridiron, he is a cool dude when he isn't on it. When I called, he said he could come to California for the picture, holiday or not, so the itinerary for the two stars was arranged. Randy would get up at 4:30 a.m. and drive to the Dallas/Ft. Worth Airport, then take a four-hour flight to San Francisco. I would then pick him up for the forty-five minute drive across the Bay to the Hyatt Hotel at Oakland Airport, the hotel where the New York Yankees were staying. For Rickey Henderson, the trip was a bit more simplified. He would have to walk two hundred feet down the hallway.

Memorial Day came, and everything was running smoothly. Randy's flight landed in San Francisco on schedule, and after we gathered his bag (containing his Cowboys uniform and helmet) at the luggage carousel, we headed up through San Francisco and across the Bay Bridge, arriving at the Hyatt right on time for the 1:00 shoot. The marketing team was there, along with the camera crew. It had taken them three hours to get the cameras and lighting set up. The shorter the time we needed for the actual shooting to take place, the better. After all, the ballroom we rented from the hotel was costing $300 an hour. Time was money, and I also had to make sure Randy made it back to San Francisco Airport for his return flight to Dallas.

Everything was right on time, and we were ready to go, minus one key component: Rickey Henderson. We waited and waited. Calls to his room went unanswered. Randy White changed into his Cowboy uniform and chatted with the camera crew. We continued to wait, and 2:00 became 2:30.

The resulting ad from the photo shoot with Henderson and White.

Finally, the door to the ballroom opened, and Henderson, followed by his posse, sauntered into the room. Rickey walked straight over to Randy White and put out his hand. Before he could say a word, the big defensive end grabbed the

Yankee leftfielder by the shoulders, put him up against the wall, and growled, "If you ever shoot a commercial with me again, you better damn well be on time!" The room was dead silent as he kept Henderson pinned against the wall. Rickey's eyes grew wide with fear—it looked like he was going to have a heart attack. Then a big smile shot across Randy's face, and he put Henderson down, announcing it was time to get on with the shoot.

There was no doubt who became the new sheriff in that room. In his Cowboy uniform, shoulder pads included, Randy White looked like the Jolly Green Giant. A real monster—with a sense of humor—and he didn't need a posse.

We were all smiles after the OLLO ad shot was taken. In the photo, left to right, are me, Rickey, Pete Zavlaris, George Sheldon, Doug Kelly, and Randy White.

● ●

Just plain good luck

"Joe wants to see you."

Those were the words Bronco Henik, the San Francisco 49ers equipment manager, said to me when I entered the locker room at the Niners training facility in Rocklin, California in August 1984.

Joe, of course, was Joe Montana; when Joe beckoned, I went. I literally ran to the back of the room and found the All-Pro quarterback sitting at his cubicle, dressing for practice. I introduced myself.

"Do you have a pair of size ten-and-a-half cleats with you?" he asked, matter-of-factly.

He didn't have to ask twice. I sprinted out to my car and had the Mizunos on his feet before he could get his shoulder pads over his head. "Feels good," was all he said. And with that the best quarterback in the NFL was heading to the practice field in "my" shoes.

I still wasn't sure what was going on, though. Joe Montana had always been an Adidas man, both at Notre Dame and in his first four years with the Niners. I asked Bronco, but he just shrugged.

I didn't want to blow a good thing, so I asked no further. I just kept delivering shoes when Joe asked for them, which was every week. And the Niners kept winning and winning—all the way to their second Super Bowl victory in the Bill Walsh era. San Francisco clobbered the Miami Dolphins, 38-16, in Super Bowl XIX, and Joe picked up another MVP award while wearing Mizuno football shoes.

Why not Adidas? It turned out to be pretty simple: Joe was pissed off at Adidas, claiming the company had violated their agreement by putting his name on a signature model shoe. Adidas claimed that the shoe was named for the Big Sky state, not the star quarterback.

And why Mizuno? Because he liked the shoe? Or the promo rep? Hardly. It was because I happened to be the first shoe rep who walked into the locker room that August morning at training camp.

So, you see, sometimes you just have to be lucky.

Signing both Montana and Elway to endorse our football line was a major step for the Curley-Bates Company. We felt that it sent a message that we could play with the big boys of the industry, most notably Nike, Adidas, Puma, and Converse. The next plan was to create an ad featuring them both. This was easier said than done, though, as trying to match their schedules was nearly impossible. Finally, a date was arranged that coincided with our sales meeting, which was going to be held at the Mondavi Winery in the Napa Valley. George Sheldon was quite a connoisseur of fine wines, and I believe he actually felt he could bring some measure of sophistication to our sales force.

On the day of the shoot, the photographers and make-up artists were all set and ready to go. Everything was perfect, minus one small detail. Montana was a no-show. We waited and waited. Phone calls to his home went unanswered (cell phones were nonexistent in those days), and we had no other way to reach him. Finally, after four hours, and with Elway just sitting around twiddling his thumbs, we gave up. I was mad as hell at Joe.

Little did I know that Montana, while missing our photo shoot, was tending to his wife Jennifer, who was ill and entering the late stages of pregnancy with their first child. He had been at the doctor's office while we were trying to call him, and since our photo was to be shot at a private studio in Napa, he could not reach us. Such are the pitfalls when working with celebrities.

The shot did take place a few weeks later in San Francisco, though not without some annoying issues, most notably that

Elway forgot to bring his game socks. While the clock was
ticking, we searched all the sporting goods stores in the city
hoping to find a pair of socks that would match the Broncos
colors. At times, the job could feel tedious.

The Mizuno ad with Elway and Montana.

In addition to the athletes and the production crew, the lady in the shot is Jennifer Montana. The couple's first child was born soon after this picture was taken.

●●●●●●●●●●●●●●●●●●●●●●●●●

High-profile athletes

Knuckleball pitchers are a zany breed. They go against all the normal things pitchers are taught: Most pitchers throw to a specific target, usually trying to get as much speed on the pitch as possible while knuckleballers basically toss the ball, and, in most cases, don't really know where the ball is going. They just try to get it somewhere near the strike zone. In many cases, they really get rolling in the later stages of their careers and, because they are not throwing so hard on every pitch, can stay in a game a lot longer—in some cases into their forties. Such was the case of Charlie Hough.

In Hough's first eight seasons in the Big Leagues, all with the Los Angeles Dodgers, he won a grand total of 49 games. In 1980, he was regularly booed by the Dodgers' faithful fans when he took the mound, usually as a middle-inning relief pitcher. He was mostly known in LA as the guy who gave up Reggie Jackson's third homerun in game six of the 1977 World Series, a monstrous blast that flew far beyond the centerfield wall.

Things began to change for Hough after being traded to the Texas Rangers halfway through the 1980 campaign. By 1982, Hough was a fixture in the Rangers starting rotation, and over the next nine seasons he won 133 games, making him one of the top pitchers in the decade for games won—all when he was in his late thirties and early forties. Charlie was one cool customer, and nothing seemed to bother him.

In July 1991, the NSGA show was being held in Chicago, and since Charlie had been traded to the White Sox during that off-season, he was a perfect candidate to come by the convention to sign autographs, which he readily agreed to do.

We planned to hook up for a couple of cocktails when I arrived in Chicago, but since the Sox were playing that night, he gave me the name of an establishment downtown and said he would get there as fast as he could after the game. Along with a couple of other Easton guys, I went to the bar and waited for Charlie. Finally, around midnight, Hough came in, grabbed a chair, lit a cigarette, and ordered a Black Russian. The stories started flying, and Charlie ordered another Black Russian while lighting another cigarette. More stories, another Black Russian, and there was always the lit cigarette. Time rolled by. Finally, after several cocktails and a pack of cigarettes, Charlie calmly looked at his watch and casually stated, "Oh, gotta go. I'm working tomorrow." Off into the night he went at the early hour of 3:00 a.m.

Hough was not kidding. He was the starting pitcher the next, I mean *that*, afternoon. He pitched nine innings, losing the close game 2-1, perhaps because he'd stayed out too late with us the night before.

Charlie Hough was one of the greatest characters in Major League Baseball—and he won over 200 games!

Later, when we were entering the McCormick Place for the autograph session, we ran into Mike Volts, Easton's sales rep for South Florida. Charlie had grown up in Miami, so I wanted to make sure they met. Now, Charlie looked older than most pro ballplayers, yet I was shocked by Voltsie's response.

"Oh, nice to meet you, Mr. Hough," he said, shaking Charlie's hand. "You must be really proud of your son. He's a great pitcher."

Smooth, real smooth. And how many ball gloves do you sell, Mr. Volts? Luckily, Charlie was a good sport and didn't get easily offended, or we may have lost a great player over that!

Another great character in baseball is Pete Rose, who has collected many names over the years: greatest hitter of all time, Charlie Hustle, gambler, and screw up. There have been more adjectives to describe Pete than for any other baseball player. One that I will add to the list is "greatest marketer." In terms of pitching a product or brand, Rose had it figured out.

In 1981 Rose was knocking on the door to surpass the great Stan Musial as the all-time National League hits leader. On August 10, in front of a frenzied crowd at the Vet in Philadelphia, Charlie Hustle rapped out a base hit to pass Stan the Man.

Following the game, Rose was surrounded by the press in the locker room when equipment manager Ken Bush yelled out to Pete that a special person was calling—President Reagan. In his typical gruff fashion, the new NL hit king told Bush, "Tell him to hold on. I'll be with him in a minute."

With that, Rose walked over to his locker, grabbed a new pair of Mizuno batters gloves, and, with the President on hold, pulled the gloves out of the package and slipped them on both of his hands. Along with the press and everyone else in the locker room, I was perplexed by Pete's actions. After all, the most powerful man in the world was waiting on the other end of the line. Rose then walked over the phone, lifted it to his ear, and said, "Hey, Mr. President, what's happening?" He sounded like he was talking to the guy next door.

The next day Rose's picture talking to the President was front-page news all across America. What logo do you think was prominently displayed on Pete's hand as he held the phone?

It was this kind of opportunity to market Pete Rose that created one of the most humorous events of my career in sporting goods. In 1985, the National Federation of State High School Associations, the governing body for high school sports nationwide, passed a new rule that effectively banned the use of metal baseball cleats. It was a silly decision with no empirical data to support such a drastic change and left coaches across America infuriated.

As mad as the coaches were, however, the new rule made things really tough for the baseball shoe manufacturers. Models had to be designed using new technology—more specifically, plastic cleated shoes. Building new molds costs the industry millions of dollars.

Once the rule was set, though, there was no turning back. We had to produce and market the new footwear, which meant that we also had to promote it, which was difficult, since no major league players were into switching from metal to plastic cleats.

Except one—Pete Rose. As the projected batting king was approaching Ty Cobb's all-time record for career hits, I asked him if he would try the new cleat that Mizuno had designed that incorporated replaceable cleats, whether metal or plastic. Understanding our need for exposure, Pete was agreeable to give them a shot.

On the evening of September 11, 1985, Pete Rose became the all-time leader in career hits, knocking a single to left field off the Padres Eric Show, and he did it wearing the new Mizuno shoe with replaceable cleats.

This was an absolute coup, but I had to get the news out to the coaching community. I wrote a short article that basically told the coaches to quit complaining; if the new style of shoes were good enough for the greatest hitter in the game, they were good enough for their high school players. A few weeks later, my article ran in *Collegiate Baseball*, and I waited for the fireworks.

They came in the form of three letters-to-the-editor in *CB*'s next edition. The first two were biting, but the third was downright brutal. The writer, a high school coach from Northern California, accused me of everything under the sun and insinuated that I had no right to pen such an article since I probably had never played baseball, much less at the high school level. It was signed by Chris Simms, head baseball coach, Campolindo High School in Moraga, California.

That did it. Now I was really pissed off! Like anyone else, I can only take so much. I went home that night, climbed into the attic and pulled out my 1969 yearbook. The next day, accompanied with a copy of the picture of the baseball team, I wrote to Coach Simms, stating he had a right to his opinion about baseball footwear. But, damn it, his accusations were out of place because right there, in the back row of the team picture in my yearbook, stood Jim Darby, senior right-hand pitcher for the Campolindo Cougars.

Talk about no respect!

Pete Rose was part of one of the most significant plays in the history of the World Series, which came in the ninth inning of game six of the 1980 fall classic. The Phillies, up three games to two over the Kansas City Royals, were two outs away from their first championship (the Philadelphia A's had last won in 1930). The Royals' Frank White, batting against closer Tug McGraw, lifted a pop foul toward the first base dugout. Closing in on the ball were catcher Bob Boone and first baseman Pete Rose. Boone, on a full sprint, reached for the ball, only to see it bang off the heel of his mitt. In a split second, Rose reached out to snare the rebounded ball to record out number two. McGraw then struck out Willie Wilson to win the Series and set off pandemonium in the City of Brotherly Love.

That catch was quite the photo-op for Curley-Bates because both Boone and Rose used Mizuno mitts. Of course, we searched everywhere for a picture of the historic play and finally found one showing the ball popping out of Boone's mitt with Rose clearly reaching out to scoop up the historic out. Our ad and poster campaign that followed stated, "When one Mizuno glove doesn't catch it, the other will."

The photo that showed the world that when one Mizuno glove doesn't catch it, another will.

The following February, at a luncheon Curley-Bates sponsored to kick-off spring training, we invited Rose and Boone to come speak. Of course, the topic that most of the reporters wanted to discuss was "the play" from the World Series. I could see Boone getting a bit hot under the collar, and when it was his turn to speak, he stepped up to the microphone and blurted out, "Charlie Hustle, my ass. It was his ball all the way. I had to run a helluva lot farther than he did to get it, and he should have called me off to begin with."

Now that's camaraderie.

On a fateful day in March 1981, I was about to jump into the Mizuno Baseball Workshop outside the Yankee clubhouse at Ft. Lauderdale Stadium. I thought we were done for the day; the technicians had put all the boxes away, and I had distributed all of the shoes and gloves into the lockers of the players we were working with.

I stopped dead in my tracks because standing in front of our glove display, checking out the wares, was none other than the most feared pitcher in baseball: Rich the "Goose" Gossage!

I had never spoken with Gossage before. All I knew was that he was big and could hurl a baseball through a wall, and with his trademark Fu Manchu, he looked mean as hell. Lord, what was I going to get myself into? I could just see myself saying, "Anything you want, Mr. Gossage. Take the Workshop—it's yours!"

The Goose had his eye on one particular glove we had hanging on the display wall. Unfortunately, it was simply that—a display. The back of this glove was composed of leather strips, sewn in perpendicular patterns. The concept was to show a glove that would allow air in to keep the hand cool. It was more of an oddity than anything else.

For some reason, though, the Goose was drawn to it. He put it on his hand. Much to my amazement, he really liked the feel and look.

"Who is this for?" Goose inquired. I explained that this particular glove was only a sample, and that no other player used anything like it. I let him know it was the only such model ever made.

"Tell you what," Gossage stated, "if you let me take this glove, I'll use it. No bullshit."

Of course, I thought it was exactly that—bullshit. After all, being the closer on the New York Yankees, and having his appearance and demeanor, the Goose was the most visible pitcher in the game. I figured it was only one glove—even if it was the only one in the world—so I gave it to him.

It turned out to be a good decision. Rich Gossage ended up using the company's ball gloves (Mizuno until the split in 1989 and then Easton) for the rest of his playing days.

The Goose intimidated hitters his entire career. Simply put, he looked like one mean S.O.B., and on the mound, he was. But there was another side to Rich Gossage that did not come across when people saw that Fu Manchu and blazing fast ball. He was one of the nicest guys ever to play the game, both before and after retirement. While most players were demanding, there were not many things the Goose wouldn't do to help me or the company—or others, for that matter.

In November 2007, Ron Davini, the Executive Director of the National High School Baseball Coaches Association, was in a panic. The BCA's annual convention was slated to be held in Oklahoma City on December 1, and it was going to be a significant event for the Association with their first Hall of Fame inductions. The problem Davini faced was that the featured speaker for the induction dinner, Bobby Winkles, was forced to cancel due to health issues. Three weeks before their biggest event, they had no speaker.

This may not seem like a catastrophic issue to most people, but to any group hosting such an event, it can really be a downer. Winkles, the former Arizona State coach and manager of the California Angels, would have been perfect, but he was out, and Davini had the pressure on his back to find someone of stature, someone who was willing to go to Oklahoma City in December.

*The Goose that laid the Golden Glove. This photo was shot for a poster
that was sent out to dealers in 1983.*

I got a call asking if I had any contacts who would be willing to come and speak. I thought of one person: the Goose. I called Rich and laid out the issue to him, and just like that, he said, "No problem." Gossage flew into Oklahoma City and gave the audience of approximately five hundred coaches, including the six Hall of Fame inductees, a speech they would never forget. No fuss, a lot of fanfare, and no fee. No fee! That is vintage Rich Gossage.

One month later, on January 8, 2008, Rich Gossage received a call that was long overdue. He was being notified that he had just been elected into the baseball Hall of Fame in Cooperstown. It was fitting!

Back in June 1989, it was quite a happy surprise when Dave Dravecky came to our office. I had not seen him since the previous September when he unexpectedly had left the San Francisco Giants to return to his native Youngstown, Ohio.

Dave Dravecky had signed a Mizuno glove and shoe contract when he was a young minor leaguer with the Pittsburgh Pirates. He really didn't come to my attention until I screwed him over. I failed to send him his spikes for the 1980 season, an oversight he distinctly let me know about in a short letter that came across my desk. Along with two pairs of spikes, I forwarded a complimentary warm-up jacket, and a new friendship was formed.

Traded to the Padres in April 1981, Dravecky rose through the ranks and was called up to the major leagues on June 8, 1982. A year later he was chosen for the National League All-Star team and pitched two innings in the mid-season classic. In 1984, he made five effective relief appearances for the Padres in the play-offs and the World Series.

In July 1987, Dravecky was traded to the San Francisco Giants, and the season was highlighted by his shutout of the Cardinals in the National League Championship Series. By the start of the 1988 season, he was the Giants opening day pitcher.

Then came problems. A sore shoulder necessitated arthroscopic surgery on June 14, disabling him for the remainder of the 1988 campaign. Unfortunately, it turned out to be more than just a sore shoulder. In September, a lump on Dravecky's arm was diagnosed as cancerous after a biopsy was performed. On October 7, 1988, in a surgical process, one-half of the deltoid muscle was removed from Dravecky's pitching arm. In addition, to kill all the cancer cells, part of the humerus bone was frozen. The doctors told him his career was finished.

Over a Chinese chicken salad that day in June 1989, you can imagine my surprise when Dave announced that he was planning a comeback even with one of the three most powerful muscles in his throwing arm missing. Dravecky had a strong disposition, though, with a ton of faith in his maker and himself. "No" was not an option. Throwing a football, he started to build strength in the shoulder, and by July he was able to throw a simulated game.

Once a week Dave came by for the Chinese chicken salad at Kincaids, a restaurant right around the corner from the Easton marketing office.

With his arm getting stronger, Dravecky made a start for the Giant's Single-A club, pitching a complete game shutout. Five days later, he pitched another complete game victory. Then, on August 4, Dravecky moved up to Triple-A Phoenix and threw another complete game, a 3-2 seven-hitter over Tucson.

We had yet another Chinese chicken salad, and it was back to "The Show" for Dravecky.

On August 10, Dravecky made his 1989 major league debut against the Cincinnati Reds in front of 34,000 fans—a large crowd drawn by the emotional drama the game presented. There were not many dry eyes in Candlestick Park when Dave jogged out of the tunnel to take his warm-up tosses. He did not disappoint; Dravecky pitched eight innings in the Giants victory, sealed when Steve Bedrosian nailed down the final three outs in the ninth inning.

Dravecky strikes out a Cincinnati Red to end an inning during his comeback game. Photo courtesy of John Green.

I guarantee that there were also no dry eyes in the offices at Easton Sports.

A week later, Dravecky made his second start, against the Expos in Montreal. They couldn't touch him through five innings. Then disaster struck. With Tim Raines on first base after a lead-off walk, Dave threw a pitch and heard a loud snap, followed by unbearable pain shooting from his left arm. The humerus bone, weakened by the cancer treatments and surgery, had snapped in half.

It was the end of a baseball career cut far too short. Unfortunately, the personal trauma continued for Dave Dravecky when, not long after that fateful day in Montreal, his left arm had to be amputated at the shoulder. The cancer had returned.

While the Giants lost a very good pitcher, the world of motivational speakers picked up one of the best ever. Dravecky has made very successful career in getting people to realize that life can be pretty darn good, no matter the adversity. He should know.

Unfortunately for me, he moved his family to Colorado Springs; I miss those Chinese chicken salad lunches.

I chatted with Dave Dravecky after the surgery to remove his left arm.

Another great guy in professional sports is Luis Gonzalez. Ask around, and everyone will say the same thing: Gonzo would give you the shirt off his back if it would help you out.

In 2001, Bob Poulos, a neighbor of mine, lost his father just before the start of spring training. I felt really bad for Bob, so I invited him to accompany me to Arizona for a couple of days. I thought getting out in the sun and calling on a few clubs could boost his spirits. It just so happened that the Arizona Diamondbacks were playing the San Diego Padres the day we were in Peoria. We were walking toward the Padres clubhouse when I heard a voice calling me from across the field, and a player came jogging over. It was Gonzo, who just wanted to say hello. Luis Gonzalez didn't even have an endorsement contract with Easton at that time—he was a Nike guy. When I told him about Bob's father, Gonzo made sure that Bob had autographs and other Diamondback goodies. The man really had a heart.

So it was really cool when, seven months later, Luis Gonzalez blooped a single over a drawn-in infield off the Yankees Mariano Rivera to win the World Series for the D-Backs. It couldn't have happened to a better guy—even if he was wearing Nike.

In January 2002, we signed Gonzo to an Easton endorsement contract and brought him to the NSGA show in Las Vegas. We were coming down the elevator with an older couple, and, as always, Gonzo was polite and charming, asking where they were from, whether they were having a good time, where they were going next, and so on. He was just being his usual "nice guy" self.

When we reached the bottom, the doors opened, and we pleasantly parted ways with the old couple. About ten seconds later, from about thirty yards away, I heard the old bitty screaming at Gonzo, letting him know, in no uncertain terms, that he should go have "intimate relations" with himself! It turns out it finally dawned on her who he was, and she was a huge Yankee fan, who couldn't stand it that Gonzo had just slain her beloved Bronx Bombers. Gonzo looked surprised but took it in stride and laughed it off.

In 2009, Jim Quinlan, Executive Director of American Legion Baseball, asked if I would do the play-by-play on the webcast of their World Series. The tournament was to take place in Fargo, North Dakota, which is not the most desirable, nor the easiest, destination. He also asked if I could recommend a couple of candidates to do the color commentary. On a whim, I reached out to Gonzo and Jeff Kent. Both star players had just retired following the 2008

MLB campaign. Even though I figured they would have some free time, I was stoked when both agreed to come.

The broadcast went really well, and I was impressed with the camera presence of Jeff and Gonzo. Most impressive, of course, is that both came gratis—no fees involved. In the world of agents and staggering fees for athletic appearances, the fact that these two all-stars gave up their time to enhance this amateur baseball event was mind-boggling.

To carry this story even to a greater depth, Quinlan told me later that the plane ticket the Legion sent to Gonzo for his trip to Fargo from Phoenix was returned unused—Gonzo paid his own way.

Broadcasting the American Legion World Series on the webcast from Fargo, ND, in 2009 with Jeff Kent.

Another shot from the American Legion World Series in 2009, this time with Luis Gonzalez.

Following the Series, Gonzo took the position of Assistant to the President of the Diamondbacks, so his appearance as color commentator was limited to that one event. Kent, in the meantime, came back to call the games in both Spokane (2010) and Shelby, NC (2011)—again, on his own time and dime. It's players like that who keep the great name of baseball alive.

CHAPTER
THIRTEEN

Bats, Part II

From 1979 through 1992, Easton controlled the adult baseball bat business in the United States. Year after year, at the College World Series, the premier event for product exposure, between 90 to 95 percent of the players were swinging the Easton brand. No coaches or schools were under any obligation or contract to swing a particular bat; the players simply preferred Easton. In addition, the Easton promotion team went hard after the business, calling on schools year-round and putting forth a huge effort at the College World Series in Omaha.

Unfortunately, nothing lasts forever.

I had expected it—seriously. In May of 1992, just as the NCAA Division One Regional Tournaments were about to get underway, Tommy Harmon, the assistant coach at the University of Texas, called our office and said, "Darbs, we've got a problem. Coach Gus is about to sign a contract with TPX."

Coach Gus was Cliff Gustafson, famed coach of the Longhorns, and TPX was the model name for bats made by the Hillerich and Bradsby Company, also known by the more popular name of Louisville Slugger.

I immediately called Cliff, and he said that, yes, it was true. "They are offering me $20,000 just to use their bat, Jim. That's a lot of money on a college baseball coach's salary."

Damn!

I asked Cliff to wait a day before signing, which he agreed to do. Then I barged into Doug Kelly's office and exclaimed, "Get the check book out!"

Our next move was to call Jim Easton at the corporate offices in Van Nuys because we needed funds, and quickly; not to mention we needed Jim's blessing to spend it.

While this call was being made, my phone was ringing off the hook. Dozens of coaches were calling, all with the same line. "Darbs, I love Easton, but this guy is offering me a lot of money and equipment if I switch my team to TPX bats." That guy offering the money was Jack MacKay.

I knew the names of the promotion people at Hillerich and Bradsby. For years we had competed against guys well-known in the industry, like Rex Bradley and Chuck Schupp. But who the heck was this Jack MacKay? I was about to find out.

The greatest self-promoter in sporting goods history, Jack MacKay, out of Mount Pleasant, Texas, convinced the higher-ups at H&B that he could take the TPX brand to new heights by buying coaches, and he started to do just that. MacKay called just about every NCAA Division One baseball coach, offering money and free equipment. And not just bats: He was offering batting gloves, ball gloves, wristbands, catchers' protective gear, helmets, caps, and t-shirts. You name it, and it was free. He quickly became the Santa Claus of college baseball.

Over the phone Jim Easton, Doug Kelly, and I set our strategy. We established an "emergency" budget to protect the number one component in our product line—the adult baseball bat. We agreed that I would offer the same program that was being offered by MacKay to college programs that I deemed to be the most important to our brand exposure. We also agreed that our absolute upper limit for any program would be $20,000 cash. We firmly believed that H&B's offers would not exceed that number.

For the next week, during the Division One playoffs and right up to the College World Series, this battle between H&B and Easton raged full tilt. I targeted and was successful in obtaining commitments from coaches that I knew were key to maintaining Easton's dominant position, including Skip Bertman of LSU, Augie Garrido of Cal State Fullerton, Mike Martin of Florida State, Cliff Gustafson of Texas, Mark Marquess of Stanford, and Jerry Kindall of Arizona. Ron Fraser, the legendary coach from Miami, was retiring, so I negotiated an agreement with Athletic Director Dave Maggard, the man who had fired Jackie Jensen, my old boss at Cal.

Some of these negotiations were tricky and almost humorous. Jim Morris of Georgia Tech called, telling me that MacKay had contacted him, but he wanted to be with Easton. What could we offer? I countered by asking how much he was looking for, and Jim immediately responded by saying $2,500 in cash plus free equipment would be just fine. Done! I told him a contract would be in the mail.

Two days later, Morris called me back, accusing me of being a no-good S.O.B. because, after speaking with other coaches, he found out some schools were being offered more than others. "But Jim," I explained, "I asked you what you wanted, and you told me. That's the number we agreed on."

"Yeah, but you should have told me you were paying other coaches more than me," he sheepishly countered.

Hmm... I'm not sure that's how negotiations work.

MacKay's goal of getting some top schools to switch to the H&B brand worked since Easton simply didn't have the budget to put every Division One program under contract. In addition, he used bullying tactics. He used those tactics on Coach Joe Arnold at the University of Florida. The Gators had a very strong following, but I had already signed Miami and Florida State when he called me with the usual information: MacKay was offering him $20,000, but he wanted to stay with Easton because of our friendship. However, $20,000 was a lot of money, and he had to put his kids through school, and so on. I really wanted to sign Florida but was concerned with amount of money being allocated to one state. I asked Joe to give me twenty-four hours to make a decision.

I agonized over the decision that night but finally came to the conclusion that I wanted Florida. So the next morning I called Arnold, like I had promised, but was jolted when he said, with a bit of a chip on his shoulder, that he had already signed with H&B.

"You said you would give me twenty-four hours!" I cried.

"MacKay threatened that if I didn't sign right away the deal was off, so I went ahead and signed their contract," Arnold stated. On that note he hung up. The war was on!

Starting around the year 2000, the regional cable television coverage for college baseball had grown, particularly in the south and mid-west. It was not unusual for the top teams in the South Eastern, Atlantic Coast, or the Big Twelve Conferences to regularly have their games televised. This was not true in the 1980s or 1990s, though; instead, the big event for product exposure and advertising rights was the CWS

(College World Series). The bat companies, most notably Easton and H&B, introduced their new bat models for the following year to the teams that made it to Omaha, hoping for maximum exposure. At the conclusion of the CWS, the sales team hit the road to call on their retail accounts to write orders for the new line. The key was the television exposure at the Series.

Easton's exposure continued to dominate, even after MacKay's push to sign up coaches. From 1980 through 1997, every bat used by the Championship team at the College World Series was an Easton, but the H&B strategy was starting to show. In 1995, the University of Southern California, swinging H&B bats, made it all the way to the championship game. Fortunately, Augie Garrido's Titans from Cal State Fullerton, led by All-American Mark Kotsay, knocked off the Trojans, 11-5, to take the crown—and keep the Easton streak alive.

We almost lost the streak again in 1996. The championship game, the 50th in CWS history, featured two premier programs: LSU, under Skip Bertman, against Miami, coached by Jim Morris (yes, the same Jim Morris, previously of Georgia Tech). LSU was an Easton school while Morris, after being hired at Miami, had accepted a huge increase from MacKay and told me to take a hike. Dollars talk, and I think the $2,500 I offered him at Georgia Tech still rankled him.

The game, aired nationally on CBS, was a classic. In a seesaw affair, Miami's Pat Burrell almost put the game away in the fifth inning when he smoked a long drive to centerfield with the bases loaded. The ball got caught up in the wind, though, and died at the fence. Back and forth the teams went until the top of the ninth when Alex Cora lined a two-out single to left to put Miami ahead, 8-7. Thus the stage was set for the most dramatic finish ever in the College World Series.

While all of this was going on, I, along with all of the Easton management team and sales force, was at our annual sales meeting being held in Vancouver, British Columbia, where the sales guys were going to see the new lines for the following year—the same line the LSU players were swinging at the game. I snuck out of the meeting room to watch the end of the game on the TV, and as LSU was coming to bat in the bottom of the ninth inning, down by a run, I was wondering what I should say to the sales force when our team lost. I was thinking something to the effect of, "Well, guys, it was a good game, and our exposure was good, but we can't win every game…" Oh, hell, this was going to be a bummer. For both LSU and us.

The LSU leadoff hitter in the bottom of the ninth ripped a double down the left field line and advanced to third on a grounder to first. The tying run was at third, and up to the plate strode catcher Tim Lanier, who had been swinging a very hot bat.

Facing Lanier was Miami freshman Robbie Morrison, a hard-throwing right-hander with a wicked slider. Morrison quickly fell behind in the count, 3-0. I thought they might walk him, putting the potential winning run at first, but it would also set up the double play possibility. "Please, please, get that tying run in," I whispered to the TV. I paced the room, going crazy with anticipation. Lanier took a strike, 3-1. Then another to put the count at 3-2. "This is the pitch," I thought. "Morrison does not want to put the winning run at first." Lanier would get a good pitch to hit.

He got a good pitch, all right—for Morrison. In fact, it was an absolute bastard: tight slider, down and away. A pitch so good that the good Lord himself couldn't have touched it. Strike Three!

I went quickly from euphoric anticipation to gloom. Two outs. The Easton streak, started in 1980, was one out from being kaput.

With the game and national title on the line, up stepped Warren Morris, the number nine hitter in the lineup, who had broken the hamate bone in his left hand and missed most of the regular season. With the way things were going, it didn't surprise me that the nine-hole hitter was up in this critical situation.

The Miami closer's first pitch was another bastard slider, cutting down and in on the left-handed batter. Morris swung and launched a line drive down the right field line, which looked like it was a base hit to tie the game up. The right fielder ran back to the wall, but, in a flash, the ball disappeared into the stands. It was gone! Morris was rounding second, fist raised in triumph, while both Cora and Burrell laid face down on the infield, pounding the turf in frustration.

On the 50th Anniversary of the College World Series, the outcome was decided by a walk-off homerun—the first time that had happened in the fabled history of the event. To use the phrase called out by the great Jack Buck following Kirk Gibson's dramatic walk-off home run in the 1988 MLB World Series, I couldn't believe what I had just seen.

By the time I took the elevator down to the meeting room, news of Morris's game-winner had already reached the sales force. It was refreshing to see middle-age men acting much younger than their years and giving each other high-fives.

Warren Morris hits the most famous home run in the history of the CWS,
using an Easton bat. Photo taken by Joe Mixan.

The Easton streak extended one more season, as LSU knocked off Alabama in the final to capture their fourth NCAA championship in the decade. It all came to an end, though, in 1998 when Southern Cal, swinging H&B bats, knocked off LSU in two straight games to advance to the championship game against Arizona State, another H&B program.

By 1998, though, there were storm clouds gathering in the direction of the NCAA and its use of aluminum bats.

Aluminum bats were first allowed for play in college and high school baseball in 1974, much to the dismay of many baseball "purists." To them it was blasphemy to let hitters use anything other than wood. In the first few years of aluminum bats, the key offensive categories of batting average, runs per game, and homeruns per game in college baseball showed increases. From 1973 to 1982, batting averages rose from .266

to .298, runs per game went from 5.07 to 6.39, and homeruns per game from .42 to ,69. The anti-metal people cried foul, claiming that the new bats were ruining the integrity of the game.

There were other points that they were overlooking. First of all, there was another change in the sport that took place in 1974: the designated hitter. The same increases in offensive output in amateur baseball were also taking place in the major leagues. The accumulative batting average for American League hitters from 1972 to 1982 increased from .239 to .264 while average runs per game and homeruns per game rose from 3.64 to 4.47 and .632 to .916, respectively. It wasn't just the aluminum bat that was causing the offense statistics in baseball to increase.

While all of this was happening, yet another change was taking place: the popularity of college baseball. Fans started packing stadiums in college towns, particularly in the South. Attendance records at the College World Series were being broken each year as the fans liked the games they were seeing.

In 1983, Easton introduced the first aluminum bat that had a barrel diameter of 2 3/4", which was the largest allowed per official baseball rules. The newer model, called the "Black Magic" quickly replaced the "Green Easton," which at 2 5/8" was slightly smaller, as the number one bat in amateur baseball.

Over the next few years the offensive categories in college baseball continued to rise. By 1985, the accumulative batting average across the country was .306, and teams were hitting twice as many homeruns as they had prior to the adoption of the aluminum bat.

Attendance records kept climbing, too.

One of the great challenges for Easton, and all of the bat companies, was designing new products each year that players desired. We simply could not supply the same bat year after year because kids demanded the latest and greatest. Each year all the companies made modifications and improvements to their bats, including new alloys, differing flex and balance points, as well multiple weights, lengths, and handle sizes. Usually, however, the biggest change, year in and year out, was cosmetic because kids liked to have new color selections to choose from. Of course, as with all consumer products, the prices of the bats steadily increased. By the early nineties, top-end bats were selling for over two hundred dollars.

While college baseball was growing in popularity, not everyone associated with the game was happy, most notably Bill Thurston, the coach at Amherst College in Massachusetts. A self-described "baseball man," Thurston also served as the secretary/editor for the NCAA baseball rules committee. In this role, he had no vote, but he certainly was an influencing factor. He was extremely vocal in his criticism of aluminum bats and their effect on the game he wanted to see on the field.

In 1992, at Thurston's urging, a meeting was held in Kansas City that involved the members of the rules committee and representatives of the bat manufacturers. Thurston stated that he was concerned that the competition between the manufacturers was creating a "bat war," and the game was going to suffer. Ironically, he neglected to point out that the key offensive categories in the 1992 season had actually dropped below the levels that existed during the early years of aluminum bat usage. Basically, he was firing a warning shot across the bow of the manufacturers.

Over the next three seasons, the offensive trends during the regular season remained constant until, at the 1995 College World Series, a new record for homeruns was set, and Thurston had his platform again. In January 1996, at the American Baseball Coaches Association convention, he told a gathering of Division One coaches that the rules committee was fed up with the "war" between the manufacturers and that the committee was going to take steps to put an end to the alleged problem he believed existed in the game. Sitting off to the side of the room, I couldn't put up with his ranting. Though I was not a coach, I wanted the truth to be known, so I stood up and challenged Thurston on the spot. What ensued was a verbal shouting match between a rules editor and bat manufacturer that left the coaches shocked and me totally red-faced and embarrassed. I was not about to let Thurston dictate how the game should be played. He certainly had a right to his opinion, but his job was to interpret the rules, not set them.

Better hitters? A hotter ball? The stars lining up? Easton's new "Redline" series of bats? I don't know the reason, but the 1997 and 1998 seasons brought increasing offensive trends in college baseball, with those in the latter season the highest in the history of the game. I knew the battle was coming when I left for Omaha in June.

On the first Saturday of the 1998 College World Series, LSU was paired up in a CBS television match-up against Southern Cal—two very good hitting teams. In the era known as "Gorilla Ball" for Skip Bertman and his Tigers from Baton Rouge, Skip's theory was to recruit the biggest, strongest kids he could find to out-muscle his opponents. Coming off back-to-back national titles, it appeared to be a pretty sound strategy.

Southern Cal jumped off to a quick five-run lead and had All-American pitcher Seth Etherton on the mound, so things looked bleak for the Easton-swinging Tigers. By the fourth inning, though, LSU had started to chip away at Etherton, and in the fifth they exploded on him. Two homeruns had already left the yard when Brad Cresse, the LSU catcher, stepped up to the plate. With the wind blowing out, Cresse crushed an Etherton fastball, far over the light standards beyond the left field wall. It was a monster shot, the longest ball I ever witnessed hit at Rosenblatt Stadium. As soon as the ball left the bat, every person in the ballpark jumped to their feet in awe; well, everyone except one person. I stayed sitting, thinking about how I was screwed.

LSU hit eight homeruns that day, and things only got worse as the week went on. By the conclusion of the Series, sixty-two homeruns had been hit, shattering the previous record The straw that broke the camel's back was the championship game, seen by a national audience on CBS. When the smoke had cleared and the dust settled, Southern Cal had finally knocked off Arizona State by a whopping score of 21-14.

Even though the last two preliminary contests leading to the championship game between Southern Cal and LSU, the two most prolific offensive teams in 1998, had played to final scores of 5-4 and 7-3, nobody remembered those games. All the anti-aluminum bat people wanted to point to was the final game. Thurston had his forum again, and this time the NCAA was smelling blood. An emergency meeting was called in Kansas City, and a public lynching was held with the bat manufacturers at the end of the rope.

The results from this meeting created nothing more than chaos. The members of the rules committee pounded the table, demanding that aluminum bats perform more like wood. Scientists who attended at the request of the NCAA could not agree how to make a non-wood bat hit like a wood bat, partly because they couldn't even agree on what wood bat they were attempting to emulate.

In the fall of 1998, college baseball coaches and the bat manufacturers were in a huge dilemma. There was no doubt that the bats used the season before would be banned, but what bats would be approved? Dyes to manufacture bats could not be made overnight, and there were lingering questions about what bats sporting goods retailers and team dealers were going to order (or what bats could they order, for that matter). It was an absolute disaster for everyone.

Finally, just before the 1999 season was about to kick-off, new standards were announced. The maximum barrel diameter of the bat was reduced from 2 3/4" to 2 5/8", which meant we had to say adios to the Black Magic. Also, the bats could weigh no less than three ounces below the length. To be more clear, if a bat was 33" in length, it could weigh no less than 30 ounces. The old rule was minus five. The final result was smaller barrels and heavier bats for 1999, and the changes worked: batting averages, runs, and homeruns decreased.

Over the next couple of years, there were additional changes to the bat standards. A maximum exit velocity was set that emulated the speed of the ball coming off the best professional-quality wooden bats, and a minimum balance point was established. By the start of the 2003 season, all the standards were in play for college and high school baseball nationwide.

The results were just what the NCAA and the National Federation of State High Schools Associations wanted. Batting averages, runs, and homeruns had leveled off to ranges below the popular "Green Easton" years of the late seventies and early eighties. College baseball continued to grow in popularity, and attendance records continued to be set year by year. The College World Series became a premier sports event, with every game being televised to a national audience, and hundreds of thousands of fans annually flooded to Omaha.

And Bill Thurston? He resigned in protest from his position of Secretary/Rules Editor. The game had grown and moved on without him.

CHAPTER FOURTEEN

The Bad

One of the benefits of being employed in the sporting goods business is having the opportunity to work around the locker rooms and stadiums, the ultimate celebrity boys' club. Serious sports fans would pay thousands of dollars to be part of the locker room scene and feel like a part of the inner circle.

Working with celebrity athletes can be like any other profession. The good can mix with the bad, especially when you feel like you're in the right place... but at the wrong time.

In September 1980, I was in Pittsburgh to call on the Pirates at Three Rivers Stadium. Gary Roderick, a friend of mine, was also making a call on the Bucs that day. Gary was an independent rep, pushing various lines to major leaguers, such as Saranac batting gloves and Brooks shoes. He was a veteran in the business and very well respected by the players.

I was standing in front of Phil Garner's locker, discussing ball gloves with Scrap Iron, when I heard a commotion on the other side of the room. Bill Robinson, the Pirate leftfielder, was absolutely airing out poor Gary Roderick; I had no clue why, and it honestly didn't matter. The locker room belongs to the players, and when one of them goes off, you just have to take it even if it is humiliating. Watching the blow-up between Robinson and Roderick left a lasting impression on me, one that left me thinking how I never wanted to be in a similar situation.

No such luck. My time came at spring training in 1983. The Mizuno Baseball Workshop was on tour, and we were calling on the Detroit Tigers at Joker Marchant Stadium in Lakeland, Florida. The opponents that day were the Dodgers, coming up from Vero Beach.

I sauntered over to the visitor's locker room and was engaged in a conversation with Dusty Baker when I heard a loud voice shout, "Get him the hell out of here!"

Profanity-laced comments are not unusual in a major league locker room, so I really didn't pay much attention.

"Get him the hell out of here!" It was much louder this time, and the room became very quiet. Dusty looked at me and asked, "Do you have a problem with Yeager?"

Turning around, I saw that every eye in the locker room was directed right at me, including Steve Yeager. It was obvious where his verbal assault was being directed. In the back of my mind, I was pondering what I did to deserve this, but I didn't even know Steve Yeager and presumed he had no idea who I was. More than that, rushing through my mind was the sick feeling of not having a clue how to handle this situation while keeping my integrity in the locker room. I looked at Dusty and his expression made it clear that I was on my own.

Sweating, I stood up and turned around to face the Dodger catcher and intelligently uttered the only thing that came to my mind: "If you have a problem, asshole, spit it out. Otherwise, shut up!"

And with that, Yeager shrugged, laughed, and headed out to the field while I stood there, shaking.

The locker room can be a tough place, and it isn't the only tough place in the sports world.

In professional sports, there are certain managers and coaches (like NFL coaches Bill Walsh and Bill Parcells, baseball managers Billy Martin and Frank Robinson, and NHL's Scotty Bowman) that commanded so much respect that I find myself getting nervous being around them. My knees shake a bit, and my mind goes blank as I search for something to say so I don't sound stupid in their presence. More than anything, I don't want to piss them off.

One time in 1998, the Detroit Redwings flew in to San Jose to play the Sharks. Arriving a day early, the team held a practice, so I went in to see the guys because there were a lot of players on Detroit using Easton products: Steve Yzerman, Nick Lidstrom, and Brendan Shanahan, to name a few. The team from hockeytown was a key exposure vehicle for the Easton brand.

Finishing my business, I was just about to leave when Paul Boyer, the equipment manager, came up to me and said, "Scotty wants to see you." Scotty Bowman?

I wound my way over to the coaches' room and knocked on the door. "Come in," a gruff voice called out.

"You wanted to see me, sir?"

"Are you the Easton guy?" he growled.

"Lord, what have I done now?" I wondered. I was afraid he would ask me a serious hockey question and then see right through me to know I had no clue about hockey equipment.

He looked menacingly at me and snapped, "Why are Nick's blades breaking so much?" He meant Nick Lidstrom and the wooden blades at the end of his Easton aluminum

shafts. In the Wings' previous game, Lidstrom had snapped a
blade on a breakaway, sending Bowman into a rage.

Think, think... What could I say that would make sense?
Then, it dawned on me: Nick did not use Easton blades. He
played with an Easton shaft but used Christian blades.

"Coach, I wish I could tell you. We've been trying to get
Nick to use our blades for years," was my smooth response,
which was enough to get me off the hook. On their next trip
into San Jose, Nick Lidstrom was using Easton blades.

While I was able to smooth-talk my way out of some
scrapes, there were times when my job just wasn't that fun,
including those times when contracts or endorsement deals
never happened, whether by simple oversight or due to
issues beyond our control. Those situations could be comical
but also flat-out frustrating. In other cases, the athlete simply
did not perform up to expectations, was injured and missed
extensive playing time, or was not able to drive up business.
At times, the athlete turned out to be a monumental pain in
the ass!

••••••••••••••••••••••••
The deals that never happened

The spring training tour for the Baseball Workshop
always concluded with our call on the Pirates in Bradenton,
Florida. We finished with the Bucs for a simple reason: Their
players had a tendency to take whatever they wanted from
the Workshop. If it was on the shelf when the players came
in, it was gone when they left. Lord knows where the ball
gloves ended up because we didn't have many players on the
club using our brand. I think a lot of cousins and friends back
home enjoyed using Mizuno pro model gloves, courtesy of

the Pirates. The scheduling was always simple—finish with Pittsburgh.

That was the way it was when we finished up in March 1983. After the last player walked out (and all of the ball gloves were gone, too), we shut the door and motored up to Tampa and our favorite Holiday Inn on Dale Mabry Avenue. It was only the best for this crew.

After getting settled in, I decided to go for my daily jog. A mile down the road I was running by the entrance to the Cincinnati Reds training camp and noticed there was a sign announcing a spring game that evening between the Reds and the Dodgers. "What the heck," I thought. "A good chance to see some players." Convincing the security guard that I really belonged, I walked onto the field and hung around the batting cage as the Dodgers were taking their pre-game hacks. Feeling a tap on my shoulder, I turned and was face-to-face with the most hay-seed looking guy I had ever seen in a baseball uniform. Inquiring if I was, indeed, the Mizuno guy, he introduced himself and said, "I was wondering, sir, if I could try one of your gloves?"

I explained that our spring training tour was over and that I had no more gloves to distribute but that I would try to send him one when I got back to California. Being the great judge of major league talent that I am, I had figured there was no way that this goofy-looking dude was going to make the Major Leagues. Not with a name like his. C'mon, really, what kind of a player could he be with a name like Orel Hershiser? My bad judgment in this case caused me to lose a potential deal before it ever got off the ground.

Many years later, in 2002, Easton needed some star power for our baseball lines. We had certainly worked with prestigious players in the past decade, like Paul O'Neill, Dave

Stewart, David Justice, and Jeff Kent. But as we were in the new millennium, we were looking for the player who would carry the brand with a name that was not only recognized in major league cities, but also one that had international appeal. In other words, we needed a player to drive sales.

The most obvious name was Barry Bonds, but he carried too much baggage. Besides, although he was arguably the best player in the game, he was not well thought-of outside San Francisco, so he was a great player but a bad pitch-man.

The next obvious choice was Alex "A-Rod" Rodriguez, the star infielder who had recently left the Seattle Mariners to sign the most lucrative contract in Major League history with the Texas Rangers. He was exactly what we needed—young, good-looking, well-spoken, popular, and, above all, a hell of a player.

A-Rod's agent was the notorious Scott Boras, so the challenge was there from the start. We knew this was going to be expensive, real expensive. The silver lining was that Boras' assistant, the man handling the endorsement negotiations, was an old friend, Mike Fiore. Fiore had played college ball at the University of Miami and had been the starting leftfielder for Team USA at the 1988 World Championships in Parma, Italy—the same venue that I had broadcast on FNN with Byron Day.

Fiore arranged a meeting in Miami between Alex, me, and Trevor Anderson, Easton's ball glove product manager, where we were given the specifications of the glove that A-Rod preferred. Two weeks later, just before Christmas, I flew back to Miami to meet with Alex at his home, bringing new samples for his approval. He gave me the full tour, including the screening room, the picture with Bill Gates, and the new red Ferrari in the garage. We were rolling!

Rolling, that is, until the start of spring training when Fiore rang me up. "There is one issue that I need to make you aware of," he said. "But it really should not be a problem."

I sighed. "OK, what shouldn't be a problem?" I asked.

"Alex signed a twenty-year contract with Louisville Slugger when he was seventeen that gave them the exclusive rights to his name on ball bats. He got a set of golf clubs for it, and they won't let him out of it."

Not a problem? Other than having Alex use our ball glove, batters gloves, and wood bats, the biggest component of the agreement was the ability to develop an A-Rod signature line of youth aluminum bats. The sales of those bats would have financed the entire contract.

No, it wasn't a problem at all—it just killed the deal. Adios, A-Rod. It probably didn't matter to him, but it was a real bummer for Easton.

Once we entered the hockey business, ice skates were a hot issue. Getting players to use Easton sticks and gloves was relatively easy, but the reception of our skates was quite another issue. Mark Howe, star defenseman for the Flyers, jumped right into the Easton skates in 1987, but that was about it. The older, traditional brands, most notably Bauer and CCM, dominated the market.

In 1998, Easton's product design manager came up with a revolutionary design for a blade holder—a concept that was sure to propel Easton into a leading position in the skate market. The entire management team was fired up as we headed for our annual meeting in San Diego, where the new skate was going to be presented to the sales representatives. When the skate was shown to the reps, there were *ooh*s and *ah*s, and we felt the excitement in the room.

Then, from a back row, one of the sales reps stood up, and in a quiet voice, asked, "How do you sharpen it?"

Say what?

The new skate had a bit of a problem: The holder did not fit on any of the traditional jigs. In other words, it couldn't be sharpened. Whoops!

There were just a few red faces in the room that day.

We never gave up, though, and by 2001 Dan Mecrones, our top pro rep, came to the conclusion that we had a hot skate. Dan had targeted Peter Worrell, the tough left-winger for the Panthers, and headed down to Florida at the start of the fall camp. Arriving in Ft. Lauderdale, he put Worrell's skates in the trunk of the rental car, where they remained overnight.

When Worrell put on the skates the next morning, he exclaimed, "These skates are hot!" Of course, Mecrones took this to mean that he really liked them. Unfortunately, Worrell wasn't describing his appreciation for the skates. He was stating they were, indeed, hot. So much, in fact, that he ripped them off his feet as fast as he could.

Poor Peter Worrell. His Easton skates had become home to thousands of red ants that had been previously living in the trunk of the car Dan Mecrones had rented the night before. They were everywhere—in the soles, toes, tongues, and even crawling out of the eyelets. Worrell was hopping around the room like someone had given him a hotfoot.

Needless to say, Peter Worrell never did become a huge endorser of Easton Skates.

•••••••••••••••••••••••••

The deals that didn't live up to expectations

Ed Farmer was the best of signs, and he was the worst of signs. This was the guy who had made me look good by being named to the American League All-Star team in 1980. Then I looked even better when he finished the campaign with thirty saves, having his name added to the list of the best closers in the major leagues.

He was good, and he had the ego to go with it.

Farmer quickly went from the guy who had called me during the Christmas holidays to mooch a ball glove to the instant celebrity demanding immediate service. On one such occurrence, Farmer called me and stated he wanted a ball glove sent to him right away. Apparently he had promised one to the son of a friend. Not thinking it was a rush, I took my time writing up the order, and the glove was shipped a few days later.

Shipping it out a few days later was not quick enough for Farmer, though. The next time I saw the White Sox on television, he was sporting a competitor's ball glove. Befuddled, I called to ask why, and Farmer, in a stern manner, told me I was slow in taking care of his needs.

I was furious and determined to get even. I sat down and penned a letter to Farmer, accusing him of being disloyal, untruthful, un-American, a communist—you name it. I took all the emotions off my sleeve and put them on paper. "Take that, brother," I thought.

Two weeks later, a letter came across my desk from Masato Mizuno, president of the Mizuno Corporation, inquiring why an American major league player named Ed Farmer wrote to him complaining about the company's American promotion manager. Inside was a copy of the vent letter I had sent to Farmer. The former All-Star stated in short verse that he would still be using the Mizuno glove if the promotion manager would simply do his job.

Who do you think was more believable to the president of the corporation? Me or the All-Star?

214   Right Off the Bat

That little episode taught me a valuable lesson I have never forgotten. Never, and I mean never, have I written anything again in anger because I know it will only come back to bite me in the end.

Mike Rozier was a sure bet. The 1983 Heisman Trophy winner ran wild in the Big Twelve Conference, and there was no reason that he wouldn't do the same in the NFL, particularly after being selected in the first round of the NFL draft by the Houston Oilers.

At least, I thought he was a sure bet. That's why I let his agent convince me that his client was worth a boatload of greenbacks, all of which went down the drain. Rozier was never able to match the exploits of his former Cornhusker teammate Roger Craig. In his eight-year NFL career, he was only able to rush for 4,462 yards—not the stuff that Heisman Trophy winners are made of. Like so many of the highly touted athletes, Rozier's unfilfilled promise was partially due to chronic injuries. It was certainly disappointing to us (not to mention expensive), but that was one of the risks we took in the marketing game.

Sammy Sosa, along with Mark McGwire, helped Major League Baseball get past the 1994 work stoppage blues when he slugged sixty or more homeruns during the seasons of 1998, 1999, and 2001. Chicks dug the long ball, and everyone loved Sammy. His ever-present smile, animated hand gestures, and signature sprint out to right field to start every game made him an icon on Chicago's North Side and the darling of baseball fans nationwide. This was the man who sat at Mrs. Clinton's side when her husband gave his State of the Union address. He was a great guy, that Sammy.

Not long after getting the news that A-Rod wasn't going to happen, I was strolling into the Cubs locker room at their spring training facility in Mesa, Arizona. Sammy Sosa was sitting at his cubicle and, as I came by, announced that he was no longer under contract with any equipment manufacturers. He requested samples and suggested that we contact his agent, Adam Katz.

Three weeks later, I flew back to Arizona with contract in hand, and Easton had their star.

At first, everything was good. Sammy hit his 500th career homerun during the first month of the season, a feat that received modest media attention. The Cubs, under the tutelage of new manager Dusty Baker, looked like a playoff-bound ball club. The dream season ended, unfortunately, under the reaching hands of Steve Bartman and the Florida Marlins, and I was about to learn about the real Sammy.

In 2003, Easton had made a financial commitment to expand the brand exposure by signing key Major League ball players. Our pro player staff, in addition to Sosa, included popular names like Javy Lopez, Luis Gonzalez, Jeff Kent, Eric Chavez, and Eric Gagne. We had some serious star power, to be sure.

It was Easton's CEO, Tony Palma, who came up with the plan to have the players come to the SGMA Super Show to put on clinics for local little leaguers, followed up by a cocktail party with selected key dealers. The idea was to position Easton as the new name in Major League Baseball.

Tony may have come up with the idea, but it was the job of the promo team to implement it, and we had to make sure the stars showed up. The calls went out. Lopez, Kent, and Gonzo were all in. But Sammy? Well, not so sure. We had no commitment from him even though the entire plan revolved around him. As good as the other players were, Sammy was "the show," and the whole promotion would lose sizzle without him.

One might think that an athlete would want to work with the company he endorses, but Sammy didn't seem to think along those lines. Through his representatives, he kept putting us off. Eventually realizing that he was obligated, per his contract, to make an appearance on behalf of the company, he agreed to come; the event was a go.

It was a go but required a mountain's worth of planning: arranging for a batting cage to be set up within the convention center, local youth leagues to be bussed in for the clinics, invitations to be sent out to dealers, and more. Most important, though, was arranging transportation for the stars. By 2004, the Super Show had relocated from Atlanta to Orlando, so we started making reservations for Javy Lopez to fly in from his home in San Diego, Gonzo from Phoenix, and Kent from Austin. For each of them, it was no sweat. We booked the commercial flights and ran them by each athlete for approval, and it was done. Simple—just as it should have been.

Sosa was living in Miami at the time, so I inquired whether he desired to fly up to Orlando or, if he preferred, we could arrange for a limousine to bring him up. After all, it was only a four-hour drive and would be much easier than having to go through the hassle of the long lines at the security checks, particularly since it was only a forty-minute flight.

Much to my chagrin, I was told that Sosa intended to fly up to Orlando for the event but that he only flew on chartered aircraft. No commercial flights for Sammy—that was apparently beneath him.

My initial reaction on hearing this news was to inform Sammy's representative that he could tell his client to take our bats and insert them where there is no sunshine. But realizing the event hinged on his presence, I sucked it up and started calling charter air companies in the Miami/Ft. Lauderdale area. Since we had already announced the line-up for the promotion and invitations had been sent out, I had no choice, which is how I explained it to Tony Palma, who was none too pleased with the new developments.

The normal first-class airfare from the Miami area airports to Orlando was about four hundred dollars; the cost of a limousine would have been about the same. I gagged when I was informed that a charter Leer Jet was going to cost us $7500 for a forty-minute flight. With no other option, I booked the Leer. I thought we were all set, but I was wrong. Payne Stewart had flown in a Leer Jet—and crashed. Sammy refused to go up in a Leer, choosing only to fly in a Gulf Stream.

You might be asking what the difference between the two is. The difference is about $5000. When I called the charter service, they explained that the Gulf Stream was a bigger aircraft, and the cost for the short flight would be $12,500! We trudged forward, though: We built it, and they all came. Javy, Jeff, and Gonzo traveled like normal people, and Sammy traveled in the Gulf Stream.

Within a year, Sosa had worn out his welcome in Chicago and soon was embarrassing himself in front of a national television audience at the congressional inquiry into steroid use by major league players.

●●●●●●●●●●●●●●●●●●●●●●●●●

The deals that fell through due to personal struggles

Each summer, buyers for many of our top retail sporting goods accounts came to our offices in Burlingame, California, to review the lines for the upcoming year. Ideally, we were able to garner initial positive booking orders, which certainly made life more enjoyable.

Of course, along with the business came entertainment, which usually meant taking the prospective buyers to a Giants ballgame at Candlestick Park. It was really fun when, as the business concluded at 5:00, we told the buyers to go the hotel to get their jackets before we headed to the ballpark. Usually, in the middle of summer, the temperature hovered between 80 and 90 degrees at our office, so the recommendation to go get coats raised eyebrows. Even though the distance between Candlestick and the Easton office was no more than ten miles, it was like going from a furnace to a freezer. There could be a thirty degree drop in temperature in fifteen minutes. No wonder so many batters struggled there—a fastball off the handle could really sting the hands when it was that cold.

One year in the mid-eighties, Doug Kelly wanted to take a very important buyer to the game and then out on the town in San Francisco. He asked me to see if a Giants player would join us, so prior to the conclusion of our presentation, I hurried up to Candlestick Park to try to convince one of the players to come along after the game. Getting little interest while making the rounds, I finally approached Frank Williams, a middle-innings relief pitcher. Shockingly, he agreed to join us. I needed a body, and though I wish I could have secured a star player, Frank would do. Besides, he was a good guy and used our ball glove.

As always, it was cold at Candlestick, but the Giants won, and the hot dogs and beer made things palatable. To make things even better, Williams pitched three innings and did well. Hooking up with him and heading up to some fine establishments in the city was going to be fun.

Too much fun, as it turned out. Hopping in and out of numerous bars, it was obvious that Frank was feeling no pain. Finally, at about 1:45 a.m., as we were heading into Planet Hollywood, I suggested that he may want to call it an evening. After all, the Giants had a game the next day. "No worries," he said. Since he had pitched three innings that night, he most likely wouldn't be called on tomorrow.

Wrong—the Giants starter was knocked out early, and the bullpen had to go to work. I was listening to the game on the radio, and when I heard broadcaster Hank Greenwald say Williams was being called into the game, I thought "Oh, no." Sure enough, Williams got lit up, and it wasn't pretty. So ugly, in fact, that the next day Williams was sent packing to the minor leagues.

I don't recall if he ever came back to the Giants. After a few years with Cincinnati and Detroit, Williams was out of baseball and headed to a sad fate. He returned to his roots in Victoria, Washington, blew through his MLB earnings and became homeless. Alcoholism and life on the streets took their toll, and he died penniless in 2009.

I realize that the one night we hung out in San Francisco wasn't the only reason for the demise of Frank Williams. I have always felt bad about it, though, and wish I had recognized that he had a problem. Rather than partying and trying to impress a customer, we should have been trying to help him.

Daryl Strawberry, another player who had personal struggles, had everything we looked for in clients: talent, looks, size, and the ability to influence people. The world was his oyster playing for the Mets in the Big Apple from 1982 through 1990. As popular as he could have been, though, the "Straw" could not shake a big problem—cocaine. He needed a new venue and a chance to clear the field, so Strawberry signed with the Dodgers in the winter of 1991. He was coming home.

I thought it was perfect. A star player was coming back to his roots with a chance to prove to the world just how good (not to mention popular) he could be in a major media market. So I took a flier and signed the Straw to a three-year endorsement contract. In one of his first public appearances back in Los Angeles, Straw attended "Daryl Strawberry Day" at Crenshaw High School, his alma mater, and the *LA Times* made it front-page news. The deal was starting to look like a good one.

Unfortunately, my idea didn't pan out. Strawberry had a decent season in 1991 but then fell back into some old bad habits. Along with those bad habits, his game sank, as did our prospects for exposure with him.

••••••••••••••••••••••••
The deals that ended due to injuries

The success that John Fulgham achieved in 1979 came as a surprise to many baseball experts. The young right-hander was brought up from AAA Louisville and promptly went 10-6 with a dazzling 2.53 ERA. There was no doubt that he was the National League Rookie Pitcher of the Year. With our contract signed, sealed, and delivered, I was looking forward to big things from John in 1980.

Things started out with a bang. In his first start in the 1980 campaign, in front of a national television audience, Fulgham shut out the defending World Champion Pittsburgh Pirates on a masterful two-hitter. Sadly, it was one of the last wins he would ever have in the big leagues. In the game against the Pirates, Fulgham blew his elbow apart. He later tried a comeback but was only able to pitch in a few more games before calling it quits. His was a career that ended far too early—for him and for us.

Bill Bordley simply disappeared. The All-American left-hander, after pitching the USC Trojans to the College World Series championship in 1978, was selected in the first round of the Major League draft by the Cincinnati Reds. However, due to his father's illness, Bordley had declared that he would only sign with a team from the west coast, closer to his Los Angeles home. Commissioner Bowie Kuhn intervened and forced the Reds, for compensation, to put Bordley up for a straw hat selection of teams approved by the talented southpaw. The winner turned out to be the San Francisco Giants.

Bill Bordley was a no-miss prospect before being shelved by an injury.

Things went south for Bordley after that. After a brief stint with the Giants in 1980, he injured his elbow and never made it back to the Major Leagues. His baseball career was over by 1982, and I lost a player that I thought was a "no miss" in providing huge exposure to our ball glove line. After that, he vanished.

At least I thought so, until one day in September 1998, my phone rang, and on the other end was Bill Bordley. He stated that he was enrolled in medical school at Stanford University, and we agreed to meet the next day in Palo Alto for lunch.

I thought it was odd that someone that age would be starting medical school, and my suspicions proved to be correctly founded the next day in a conversation over deli sandwiches. Bordley showed me his registration card for med school and even described his classes to me. Even with that, things just didn't seem to add up, and I finally looked him in the eye and inquired what the hell he was really doing there. After staring around the room to make sure we couldn't be heard, Bordley whispered, "I'm in charge of the Secret Service detail guarding Chelsea Clinton here at Stanford." So there it was.

Bordley had experienced quite a ride after his baseball career came to a sudden halt. He went back to USC to obtain his undergraduate degree, worked a couple of jobs in the business world, and finally ended up joining the Secret Service.

Of course, many of his duties were classified and will go untold. One adventure he did share with me was the day he was standing watch outside the Oval Office when a young brunette intern tried to enter, claiming she had an appointment to see the President. Lacking the appropriate credentials, Bordley denied her entrance. Just then, the door opened, and President Clinton waved for the young lady to enter; she obviously had the right credentials for President Clinton. Her name was Monica Lewinsky.

Bordley left the Secret Service following the Clinton administration and went to work for the National Security Administration. Life can take turns and twists, and many times can come full circle. Such is the case for Bill Bordley, for in November, 2011, he was appointed by Commissioner

Bud Selig to the position of Vice-President/Head of Security for Major League Baseball. While he may not have gained security by playing baseball, he is security for the sport.

CHAPTER
FIFTEEN

The Politics of Wood and Non-Wood Bats

In the July 24, 1989, edition of *Sports Illustrated*, noted columnist and broadcaster Peter Gammons wrote,

> Pressed by economic forces, the low minor leagues are likely to begin playing with aluminum bats within two years. By the turn of the century even the majors will probably have put down the lumber and picked up the metal. Like it or not, the crack of the bat is inevitably being replaced by a ping.

Whoa there, Peter—not quite. All these years later, the "ping" is no closer to the majors than it was in 1989; however, the controversy of wood and non-wood bats continues to rage across the U.S., even after strict regulations have been put into play by the amateur baseball associations and leagues.

"Ping," the sound associated with aluminum bats, is slowly being replaced by the more accepted "crack" of the ball coming off composite bats, but that has not stopped the wood traditionalists in their quests to have all non-wood bats banned.

The contingent against non-wood bats always points to safety as the number one issue. They claim the ball comes off the non-wood bat at exit speeds that do not give pitchers a chance to protect themselves. However, all data that has been collected by the major amateur associations and leagues demonstrated that, in addition to being a "safe" sport, injuries due to batted balls have, in reality, been reduced since performance standards have been set on non-wood bats. Little League International, Inc., the largest baseball organization in the world, reported that injuries to pitchers due to batted balls decreased dramatically since 1992, which was the year Little League and the manufacturers agreed to limit the performance of non-wood bats to the then current manufacturing specifications while an acceptable performance standard was being developed. That standard, called the Bat Performance Factor (BPF), was later instituted, and injuries to pitchers continued to decline. The insurance companies underwriting the policies for the PONY and Babe Ruth baseball organizations reported that premiums were not higher for leagues using non-wood bats because no higher risk of injuries existed.

In 2002, Jack MacKay, our old friend, petitioned with the Consumer Product Safety Commission to issue a rule requiring that all non-wood baseball bats perform like wood bats. MacKay had left his old employer, Louisville Slugger, departing under somewhat suspicious circumstances, and was engaged in running his own wood bat company. His petition was denied. The CPSC wrote,

> You [MacKay] have provided no information, nor is the commission aware of any, that injuries produced by balls with non-wood bats are more severe than those involving wood bats.

In 2007, the National Federation of State High School Associations funded a test that was conducted by Illinois State University. The study followed 32 high school teams in more than 400 games and found little difference in the number of injuries when wood bats were used versus non-wood bats.

As with all activities, injuries in baseball can, and do, happen. Though extremely rare, in baseball there is a double standard. When a pitcher is injured by a ball struck by a non-wood bat, people tend to point to the bat; however, when a pitcher is injured by a ball hit off of a wood bat, well, that's just part of the game.

For example, in 2001, Billy Hughto, a high school pitcher in Massachusetts, was severely injured when struck by a ball hit off an aluminum bat. His father went on a crusade to have aluminum bats banned. At about the same time, Bryce Florie, a pitcher on the Red Sox, had his eye shattered by a line drive off the wood bat of the Yankee's Ryan Thompson. A few years later, a ball struck off a wood bat crashed into the face of Stanford's Erik Davis, who was pitching in the Cape Cod summer collegiate league. Davis had to be airlifted to a hospital in Boston, where he went through two surgical procedures to save his eyesight. In the Florie and Davis incidents, not one word was uttered about the bats.

In July 2003, Brandon Patch, a left-handed pitcher from Miles City, Montana, tragically died after being struck by a line drive off an aluminum bat during an American Legion game. There was an immediate cry by the anti-aluminum contingency to have the bats banned in the state, and a bill was drafted by Representative Gary Matthews of Miles City. Not much later, a high school player in Utah died after being struck by a ball hit off a wood bat while he was throwing batting practice. Not a word was mentioned about the danger of wood bats. In an incident that garnered national attention, Mike Coolbaugh, first base coach for the Colorado Rockies Double A team, was tragically killed by a line drive in July 2007—off a wood bat. Yet again, not a word about the bat.

The Montana situation was challenging. House Bill 588, along with House resolution HJ19, were first heard by the Business and Labor Committee, which voted "no" on the bill but affirmative on the resolution. It didn't help that the author of the bill, Gary Matthews (D), Miles City, was the Speaker of the House at the time. There was another hearing, this time in front of the Senate Business, Labor, and Economic Affairs Committee, chaired by Democrat Carolyn Squires. Representing the SGMA Baseball/Softball Council, I spoke at this hearing and stated to the Committee that many of the assertions made by Representative Matthews were not accurate. For example, in the bill and resolution, he had written,

> WHEREAS, nationwide responsible baseball organizations and governmental bodies have found that non-wood bats that increase the velocity of batted balls beyond the ability of defensive players to react to them have resulted in a rising rate of injuries and that this places our children, particularly those of high school age, in an unacceptable risk of injury.

Contrary to the statement, injuries in amateur baseball had not increased. Injuries, in reality, had decreased.

Representative Matthews also wrote,

> WHEREAS, the wood bat is forgiving in that it breaks, and aluminum bats repel the baseball at velocities that exceed human reaction time.

In this assertion, Representative Matthews was partially correct. Wood bats do break and, in some instances, have become missiles flying out on to the field and striking players. For instance, in 2005, Rick Helling, pitching for the Brewers Triple A club in Nashville, had the barrel end of a broken wood bat impale in his arm. On May 4, 2006, pitcher Clay Hensley of the Padres was struck in the back of the head by the broken end of Andre Ethier's wooden bat. And, of course, the most famous incident of a broken wood bat occurred during the 1977 World Series when the Dodger's Steve Yeager was injured as a piece of teammate Bill Russell's broken bat hit him in the neck, piercing his esophagus. Yeager had nine pieces of wood taken out of his neck in 98 minutes of surgery. Representative Matthews was correct in his statement: Wood bats do break.

However, the second part of this "WHEREAS" was off-base. Representative Matthews may have been an honorable man and a fine politician, but he was not an expert in human reaction time. There exists no data that corroborated Representative Matthews' statement on reaction time.

In my appearance before the Senate Committee, I pointed out these inaccuracies as the bill and resolution were written. At the conclusion of the hearing, I was startled to hear Chairwoman Squires say, "Mr. Darby, will you please come back to the podium." Nervously, I shuffled back up to the front of the witness stand.

"What gives you the right to come to our state and accuse the Speaker of the House of lying?" she asked.

Chairwoman Squires' question stunned me, and for a second I groped for an answer. Finally, I said, "Madame Chairwoman, I never stated that Representative Matthews was lying. However, I do believe that he has been misinformed."

That did not get me totally off the hook. Chairwoman Squires followed up with, "Sir, I do not want you leaving our state until I have, in writing, why Representative Matthews' assertions are incorrect."

I retired to an empty room next to the hearing room and hand-wrote the truth for the Senate Business, Labor, and Economics Affairs Committee. After that, I was finally free to go home.

•••••••••••••••••••••••••

No politician was more pervasive on this subject than James Oddo (R), Minority Leader of the New York City Council. In 2001, he posted a bill that proposed banning the use of metal bats for all play within the city limits of the Big Apple and was ready to push for a committee hearing on the bill when his plan was detoured by the events of 9/11. He then waited for a time that suited his purposes, and, in September 2002, I found out that Councilman Oddo's bill was going to be heard by the Youth Services Committee, chaired by Democrat Lewis Fidler of Brooklyn.

Why was Oddo so adamant about pushing the bill? Good question. I made a number of calls to the area newspapers to inquire if there had been an injury in his district but came up empty. Regardless, it was a serious issue in the world of amateur baseball. A politician claiming a product is unsafe, even if he had no facts, was not something to ignore. The top leaders of amateur baseball came to testify against the bill.

The hearing was nothing more than a circus. Oddo made sure that the network news cameras were on when he went on his tirade, accusing the heads of the amateur associations of being in concert with the bat manufacturers, claiming that we were all part of a cartel to squeeze millions of dollars out of hard-working American families. Once he was finished, and the cameras were gone, the leaders of the amateur associations had their opportunity to address the committee. Speaking on behalf of "bat of choice" were Paul Seiler, Executive Director of USA BASEBALL; Abraham Key, President of PONY Baseball; Joe Smiegocki, Vice-President of Babe Ruth Baseball; and Steve Keener, President and CEO of Little League Baseball, the largest amateur baseball organization in the world. Over three million kids play Little League ball worldwide each year, so he was representing quite a large group of athletes.

Keener got right to the point in his testimony, challenging Fidler as to the validity of Oddo's statements. He questioned why those testifying were not required to take an oath to tell the truth. The Chairman stated that taking an oath was not the practice at City Council committee hearings, to which Keener quipped, "Well, it should be because there were many statements made earlier by Councilman Oddo that were not true." It was a very powerful statement, one very embarrassing to Oddo—an embarrassment he would not forget.

The bill died in committee.

That was not the last we heard from Councilman Oddo, however. In 2004, he again submitted a proposal to have metal bats banned from play in New York City. Again the bill was given to the Youth Services Committee.

The press was made aware of Oddo's bill, and I was contacted by one of the producers of *Outside the Lines*, a sports talk show that aired on ESPN. They wanted to do a live interview, pitting me against Councilman Oddo in a half-hour debate. Of course, this forum was exactly what Oddo wanted. He could portray himself as the hero who was going to protect the nation's youth from the big manufacturer whose only interest was huge profits. It would be a no-win situation for me or any other bat manufacturer. I declined the offer but suggested Steve Keener of Little League, who agreed to the interview along with Oddo. It was no contest. Keener calmly laid out the facts and confidently demonstrated with clear data that the use of approved non-wood bats was safe for amateur baseball players. Oddo had no facts and became very flustered, continually referring to the "tradition" of the game and the "bat cartel." He simply could not address safety, which was the key issue. Keener easily won the debate.

James Oddo is not a man who takes kindly to being embarrassed on national television. In a letter addressed to Mr. Jim Easton, written on New York City Council stationery, dated August 23, 2004, Oddo wrote,

> It is a shame that Easton chose not to participate in a discussion of the safety of metal bats on ESPN's *Outside the Lines* last week. It is disappointing that Jim Darby and Easton picked up their bats and went home. Apparently, that is where you left your balls, as well… I will be holding a second hearing on my legislation to ban metal bats in New York City this fall and we are going to vote the bill into law. Show up, don't show up. It really does not matter. I will do what I believe is right and you can all go to hell.

Oddo's second attempt to ban metal bats never made it to a committee hearing. However, the rhetoric in his letter to Jim Easton clearly demonstrated the bullying personality he had. He wasn't simply going to fade away; the man was on a personal political crusade.

Sure enough, on October 12, 2006, we were notified that Oddo had submitted another bill, and a hearing was scheduled by the Youth Services Committee, chaired by Lew Fidler, for October 23. There was a slight change in the wording of the bill because this time Oddo had narrowed down his target audience, only trying to ban the use of metal bats for high school play. His reasons for narrowing it down to high school were simple: Oddo did not want to have any serious opposition from the amateur baseball organizations or parental groups. He knew from his earlier experiences that there was no data to support his allegations that metal bats were unsafe, so he chose the path of least resistance. Even though they tried, the high school coaches of New York City and the Public School Athletic Association were not in a position to build a strong lobby. At the hearing, Martin Oestreicher, Chief Executive of School Support Services in the Department of Education for New York City, testified,

> We do not support this legislation because we do not believe the banning of aluminum bats will enhance the safety of our baseball players… The PSAL operates under the rules of the National Federation of State High School Associations. This group represents the overwhelming number of high school sports organizations throughout the country. We have worked closely with the Federation and have sought its advice on this issue as it has data on high school baseball throughout the entire country. It is the Federation's opinion that aluminum bats do not represent a significantly greater risk than wooden bats. With very few exceptions, aluminum bats are used by high schools and colleges throughout the USA.

Diplomatically, Mr. Oestreicher was telling the Youth Services Committee that the bill had no credence. The use of approved metal bats did not constitute a safety risk to the high school players in New York City.

Oddo was desperately attempting to get scientific data to support his claim. Six days prior to the hearing, Dr. Rick Greenwald, a noted scientist who had done extensive research on the performance of wood and aluminum bats, received an email from Steven Matteo, Councilman Oddo's Chief of Staff, that stated,

> I am writing you because the Youth Services Committee of the NYC City Council will be holding a hearing on the bill to ban aluminum bats in high school play (in NYC). The hearing is scheduled for next Monday October 23, 2006. While I apologize for the late notice, I am hopeful that you are able to lend a hand to the hearing, through live testimony or submitted written testimony. We are currently in need of scientific information that states that aluminum bats outperform wood bats.

Currently in need of scientific information? This email was sent six days before the hearing and four years after Oddo had first brought his legislation to the Youth Services Committee.

In his response to Matteo's request, Dr. Greenwald wrote,

> I would oppose any statement that linked such a limitation on using non-wood bats to injury, simply because there are no scientific data to support this contention. This is an important and overlooked point. I urge Councilman Oddo to consider this as you move forward.

Sadly, Councilman Oddo decided not to share this information with the committee, even though he had openly solicited the expertise of Dr. Greenwald.

I thought that Oddo's bill, which was opposed by the public and private high schools and had no scientific data to support it, would go nowhere. I was wrong.

I learned in the real life course of Political Science 101 that legislation does not necessarily get passed on merit but on political favors. In this case, that political favor came in the persons of Lew Fidler, Chairman of the Youth Services Committee, and Christine Quinn, Speaker of the City

Council. Fidler, in a complete reversal from his position at the first hearing in 2002, made it clear at the 2006 hearing that he was going to support Oddo. It was so blatantly slanted, in fact, that Fidler used a wooden bat as his gavel to call the hearing to order. I knew immediately that we were in trouble. The fix was on.

Ugly politics was raised to a new level when it became obvious that Christine Quinn was also throwing her support behind Oddo's bill. The leaders of amateur baseball in the U.S., including Paul Seiler, Steve Keener, Abe Key, and top local New York baseball people, requested an audience with Quinn to explain to her why the bill had no merit. The meeting was held at City Hall in November, and Quinn looked completely disinterested. With Fidler and Oddo seated next to her, she spent the majority of her time giggling with Oddo and answering emails.

I spent the months of November 2006 through March 2007 lobbying as many members of the City Council that I could. Nearly every person told me the same thing: Oddo's bill was frivolous and shouldn't even be considered by the City Council. Too many times I heard them say, "Oh, that's just Jimmy."

Frivolous or not, individual members of the City Council were not keen to go against the Speaker. After all, she controlled what legislation would be brought up for committee hearings; therefore, it was not a total surprise when, in March 2007, the bill passed by a vote of 43-6 with two abstentions. Opposition by Mayor Bloomberg wasn't enough, as the Council had enough votes to override his veto.

Politics and baseball are a bad mix.

From 2002-2008, politicians from no fewer than ten states reviewed the case of non-wood bats. In each instance, the amateur baseball organizations all fought against any political involvement in this issue. And, in each case, these organizations made it clear that there is no more chance of a severe injury using approved non-wood bats than there is using wood bats.

While safety is the sexy argument, particularly for politicians, there are many baseball purists who disdain the use of non-wood bats because they believe the game was invented with wood bats, and that's just the way it should be played as a matter of tradition. How long does a product have to be used before it becomes "traditional"? Aluminum bats were first allowed for play in Little League ball in 1971 and by the NCAA and National Federation of State High School Associations in 1974, which happened to be the same year that the designated hitter was first used in high school and college baseball. Two whole generations of American kids have grown up using non-wood bats. Virtually every current player in the major leagues today developed his swing and honed his skills using aluminum or composite bats.

Statistically, the amateur game has never been more exciting or consistent. Since 2003, the first season of the current bat standards set by the NCAA, offensive statistics for college baseball have been similar to those for the years 1979-1982, which was the era of the famous "Green Easton" bat. And no one was complaining about non-wood bats during the 1979-1982 seasons. I know because I was there.

Ben Hines was the head baseball coach at Laverne College for over twenty years before moving on to serve as a hitting instructor for the Los Angeles Dodgers and Houston Astros. He is a member of the American Baseball Coaches Association Hall of Fame. In the 1989 article regarding aluminum bats, Hines told Peter Gammons,

The first thing in hitting is having the confidence that you can hit. The aluminum bat gives you that. Kids now don't grow up with the fear of hurting their hands. It's made a tremendous difference, especially to kids living in the North. With a wooden bat, it's nearly impossible to hit on cold days until mid-May, and by then most college and high school seasons are over. With an aluminum bat, you can hit no matter what the temperature. Between the cost factor and the weather factor, aluminum bats are allowing a lot more kids to play. Isn't that good for the game?

Amen, brother.

CHAPTER
SIXTEEN

Job of a Lifetime

Throughout my career I have had the opportunity to be around some of the greatest athletes of my generation and past generations. What I wouldn't have given to have had a video camera to record those moments! The following stories left a lasting impression on me, and I only hope my words here capture some of the fervor and excitement that I had felt at the time.

•••••••••••••••••••••••••
Hanging out with the greats

Nineteen eighty-four was a magical year for the faithful Chicago fans. Their beloved Cubs were finally in the post-season for the first time since 1945. No true Cub fan will ever forget the 1984 campaign and the performance of their heroes, including Rick Sutcliffe, Leon "Bull" Durham, Andre Dawson, and, of course, future Hall-of-Famer Ryne Sandberg. Harry Caray was in earthly heaven, and the Budweiser was flowing in the Windy City.

Facing the Cubs in the National League Championship Series was the upstart San Diego Padres, managed by the crafty Dick Williams, with General Manager Jack "Trader" McKeon pulling the strings behind the scenes.

That year was my first trip to the friendly confines of Wrigley Field, and I found it to be everything it was built up to be. There really is magic at Wrigley—the neighborhood, the smells, the traffic, the bars… everything about the place is magic. The aura transcends generations. And here I was, standing behind the cage, watching the two squads swing through batting practice on a warm, sun-filled afternoon, during the first October baseball on the North Side in thirty-nine years.

Ten minutes before game time, I was still down on the field. Actually, I was sitting in the Padres dugout, shooting the breeze with Goose Gossage, Dave Dravecky, and Mark Thurmond. It was like we were just passing the time of day, as if we were all on a coffee break. Looking around, I wanted to freeze time right then and there.

My moment in baseball heaven came to an abrupt end when, just prior to the team introductions, an official-looking guy spotted me and pointed to the dugout exit. I was out of there but will cherish that moment forever.

During one spring training, I happened to be at Dodgertown, working the players during the break between the morning workout and the afternoon game. Players were hanging out and moving between the training room and the food spread, doing their best to avoid the hoard of reporters that continually followed the Dodgers during the Lasorda years.

Finally, it was game time, and the locker room emptied out, leaving only Dave Wright, the equipment manager, and me. Being the true gentleman that he was, Dave invited me to help myself to the spread on the lunch table which, coincidently, was directly across from Lasorda's office. One rule of thumb for people in the sporting goods business was to never, ever take food from the major league spread without an invite. Players, for whatever reason, deemed that to be their personal stash; unless invited, we kept our hands off. Once given the nod, though, it was fair game, and this was some serious grub. Major league spreads are definitely not chicken-feed.

While I was stacking my plate with hot soup and deli delights, who should walk in to take part in the dining experience but two of my boyhood idols, Don Drysdale and Sandy Koufax. Here we were, just the three of us, in a chance meeting over cold cuts and chicken soup. I was so awestruck being near Sandy Koufax that my hands shook as I handed him a plate. Even more amazing was that he actually wanted to know who I was and what brought me to an out-of-the-way place like Vero Beach, Florida. For about half an hour, I had the pleasure of being around two of the most dominant pitchers of their era. The excitement of the moment left me unable to remember a single thing we talked about. Like I said, I'd give anything to have had a video camera.

In February 1987, the Mizuno crew was working the Giants spring training camp at Indian School Park in Scottsdale, Arizona. It was an abnormally warm day, even for Arizona. I was working the players in the locker room when they all headed out to the field for stretching, so I went back to the Baseball Workshop, parked right outside the entrance. Sitting inside, getting out of the sun and away from the pesky reporters, were three of the "honorary" coaches: Willie Mays, Willie McCovey, and Joe Morgan. They were joined by former major league star Ron Fairly, then a member of the Giants broadcast team. The three Hall of Famers and designated voice stayed in the shade of the Workshop for over an hour, relaxing and enjoying the cuisine of hot coffee, donuts, and blueberry muffins. Most of the conversation revolved around the old days, which meant playing against the rival Dodgers and their old nemesis, Don Drysdale. Mays, in his high-pitched, scratchy voice, crackled about how Dodger Don knocked him down every time he came to the plate. It was expected. McCovey just nodded, although it is well documented that Big Stretch used to eat Drysdale for lunch.

Willie McCovey, Willie Mays, and Joe Morgan share a few stories in the Baseball Workshop. I don't think they were laughing so much when talking about facing Don Drysdale.

Not to be outdone, Fairly, who spent most of his career with the Dodgers, countered that Big Don knocked him down during batting practice. Talk about tough—he had to face chin music during batting practice and from a teammate, no less. "As Don saw it, we were going to get it during the season, so we might as well get used to it," he explained, laughing.

Morgan added a story of his own: "Once, when I was a rookie with the Astros, we were playing in Philadelphia, and Gene Mauch was the manager of the Phillies. As I stepped into the box, I could hear Mauch yell out to the pitcher to knock me down because he wanted to know if I could hit from my back."

Baseball can be a rough business, and no pitcher, including Drysdale, evoked toughness as did the great Hall of Fame pitcher Bob Gibson.

One day in 1994, I was sitting in the dugout at Al Lang Stadium in St. Petersburg, Florida, as the Cardinals stretched in center field. Sitting right next to me were two Cardinal legends, Gibson and the great base-stealer, Lou Brock. I had known Brock for a while, and he was gracious enough to introduce me to Gibson. As you may imagine, the topic of discussion was centered around pitching inside or, as Gibson put it, the lack thereof in the game. In his eyes, it was a lost art. Pitchers own the plate, and hitters should have fear when they stand in the box.

I asked about baseball fights and they both laughed. "Usually nothing more than shoving matches," they both quipped.

"I'll tell you what I did," Brock stated. "When a fight broke out, and everyone started charging the mound, I looked for the fattest guy running in from the other team's bullpen. I figured by the time he reached the mound he would be gassed, and I could drill him."

Sound logic!

Being around some of the great names of baseball was never a bore, and being around Pete Rose was no exception.

I had the pleasure of hanging out with the all-time hit king on numerous occasions.

At 11:30 on the night of September 11, 1985, I was sitting in Pete's office, waiting for the king to come back into the Cincinnati Reds locker room. Three hours earlier, Rose had knocked an Eric Show fastball into left field to finally pass Ty Cobb and become the all-time hit leader in Major League Baseball history.

With Pete Rose in his office the night he broke Ty Cobb's all-time hit record.

For two weeks before that, I had been traveling with the Reds. As the promo rep for Mizuno, I had to be sure that Rose was using all of the newest and greatest products when he finally got the big knock. After all, every picture of that moment would go down in history.

So there I sat while Pete spoke with the media, including a long list of networks like ABC, NBC, CBS, ESPN, and CNN, until he finally came in to his office. "What are you doing?" he asked.

"Well, I just wanted to congratulate you one more time before I took off," I responded.

"Bullshit," Pete snapped. "Let's go get some dinner." Believe me, he didn't have to ask twice.

Pete had made arrangements at the Precinct, a restaurant along the Ohio River, to have a table ready. As we drove out of the parking lot at Riverfront Stadium, he said, "Joe's coming with us." Joe who? Oh, just Joe Morgan, former Hall of Fame second baseman for the Reds.

As we entered the Precinct, the late night diners and drinkers stood to give a rousing ovation. And I kept thinking that they must be asking themselves, "Who are those two guys with Jim Darby?"

In early February 1987, Pete Rose was the featured speaker at a hot stove dinner to help raise funds for Hancock Junior College in Santa Maria, California. I drove Pete to the dinner and was the designated chauffeur to get him to the hotel following the proceedings. As we were leaving the auditorium where the dinner was held, an older gentleman who had also been on the dais that evening hit us up for a ride. His name was Leo Durocher: Leo the Lip, infamous former manager of the Brooklyn Dodgers, New York Giants, and Chicago Cubs. The Lip was also the shortstop on the 1934 St. Louis Cardinal ball club that was known as the Gas House Gang. I couldn't believe my luck. Here I was with arguably the two most controversial personalities in the history of Major League Baseball.

The three of us spent most of the evening and early morning back at the Holiday Inn (remember, this was Santa

Maria) spinning baseball stories. At least Pete and The Lip were spinning stories. I just sat there most of the evening in awe, wishing that I had a camera to record it all.

Do you know who had the honor of being Babe Ruth's roommate when the Bronx Bombers were on the road in 1927? None other than rookie shortstop Leo Durocher. As the Lip put it, though, he never saw much of Ruth. The Babe, apparently, had other places to hang his hat.

Another intriguing moment of the evening occurred as we were entering the lobby of the Holiday Inn. Pete strode right up to the front desk and requested that extra televisions be brought up to his suite, which I thought was a bit odd. "But," I thought, "he's Pete Rose, so he can do anything he wants."

A few minutes later, three extra televisions were hooked up in Pete's suite. As soon as they were up and running, Pete started switching channels until he was able to find the college basketball games being aired. I remember thinking to myself, "Huh, Pete must really be a big fan of college basketball."

Even before I began my career with Easton, I had built friendships with athletes that I have kept over the years. When I accepted the position of pitching coach at St. Mary's College in January 1975, about forty hopefuls gathered at our first practice, including a gangly, goofy-looking kid who looked like a fish out of water. Putting it bluntly, he just did not look like a college baseball player. Spying the roster sheet, I noticed he had signed up as a pitcher, and his name was Tom Candiotti.

We split into positions, and Candiotti took the mound to show off his stuff. Lord, it didn't look like he could pitch at all. He couldn't break a pane of glass with his best heater. On the other hand, it looked like he had a decent breaking ball, and since we were in need of arms for the junior varsity team, he made the cut.

By mid-season, the goofy right-hander had been so successful getting junior varsity hitters out that we moved him up to the varsity. He kept getting hitters out with the big curveball, and toward the end of the season he had moved up to number one on the depth chart.

Two things were obvious about Candiotti: He had a boatload of confidence in his ability, and he was a hard worker. There were many evenings we stayed late after practice working on new pitches. Most notably, he worked on the knuckleball, which he didn't throw regularly in games. Even then, it was obvious that he could throw a good one and just needed to build the confidence to throw the knuckler in tight situations.

The last weekend of the season found the St. Mary's Gaels flying down to Southern California to take on powerhouse Pepperdine, the number one team in the league. We were two games out of the lead with these three games looming, so the Friday game was pivotal. It featured a match-up of our goofy freshman against Pepperdine's ace, future Cy Young winner Mike Scott. In one of the most exciting collegiate games I ever witnessed, Scott out-dueled Candiotti, 2-1, with both starters going the distance.

I left St. Mary's at the conclusion of the season while Candiotti went on to a stellar four-year career with the Gaels, a career that led him into the school's Hall of Fame. Following his collegiate career, Candiotti went on to hone his knuckleball skills, working his way through the minors. Finally, in 1986, he made it to the Major Leagues for good, hooking on with the Cleveland Indians. He was the Tribe's leading pitcher for the next six campaigns, averaging thirteen wins per season. In December 1991, as a free agent, Candiotti signed a four-year, fifteen million-dollar deal with the Los Angeles Dodgers—a huge agreement for that time.

Going over the knuckleball grip with Tom Candiotti prior to an Indian/ A's game at the Oakland Coliseum.

It was right around that time that I received the phone call. "Darbs, this is Candy. I need a favor."

"Anything you need," I replied. "What can I do for you?"

His reply stunned me. "I need you to testify at my divorce trial." *Say what?*

Tom was married to the former Debbie Wellman, whose father Gene was a well-known junior college baseball coach in the Bay Area. Her brother, Brad, had played eight seasons in the Major Leagues, splitting time between the Giants, Dodgers, and Royals. She and Tom had two sons, and, for all I knew, their marriage was rock-solid. Obviously, I didn't know much.

Debbie was suing Tom for divorce, citing irreconcilable differences. She claimed that since she had been the major bread winner for the family while he was honing his knuckleball skills in the minor leagues, she was entitled to half of his earnings for the rest of his career, which, of course, now included the fifteen million he was guaranteed from the Dodgers.

How did I fit into this? I was asked to testify that I worked with Candiotti on his knuckleball before he ever met Debbie. After swearing to tell the truth, the whole truth, and nothing but the truth, that is exactly what I told her attorney and the court.

"Can you tell the court an exact time when you and Mr. Candiotti worked on the knuckleball?" he inquired, with an accusing smirk.

"No, sir," I replied, "I cannot remember exact dates. But I certainly do remember working with Tom on his grip and release point for the pitch."

He then pulled a baseball out of his suit pocket and demanded that I show the court how to grip the knuckleball, which I proceeded to do. I then explained that Candiotti held his knuckleball with a somewhat different grip than I did.

"Why is that?" he asked.

"Because he throws a better one than I do," I answered, bringing a chorus of chuckles within the courtroom.

Candiotti won—and lost. He ended up having to give Debbie a quarter of his lifelong earnings, not the half that she was demanding. As for me, I received a free beer from Tom after the hearing along with a lifelong friendship.

As a side note, that gangly, goofy kid who walked on at St. Mary's ended up winning 151 games in his distinguished major league career.

Around the same time I was getting the call from Candiotti, I got another call from a friendly voice.

"Darby, what are you doing for lunch?" the gruff voice at the other end of the phone asked.

Answering that I had nothing planned, the caller said, "Well, John's in town, and we're going over to the Sundance, so come join us."

The caller was Jack Elway.

Jack Elway being filmed doing a feature on the benefits of Easton football pads.

Nobody in their right mind would turn down an invitation from the Elways because it was always too much fun. That day at the Sundance restaurant in Palo Alto was no different—lunch started at noon and ended at eight. I feel pretty fortunate to be able to call the Elways friends.

Once, during a game between the Broncos and Forty-Niners, I was able to garner a couple of field credentials.

Standing behind the Broncos bench, I watched as the offense came off the field after going three and out. John Elway spotted me and, instead of going to the bench, walked over to where I was standing and, in a voice only I could hear, stated he needed a new set of Mizuno golf clubs. No surprise—that was John. He may have loved football, but he also loved having fun.

Jack took his son's career very seriously. The night before the 1990 Super Bowl, a game featuring John's Broncos against the Forty-Niners, Sarah and I had dinner with Jack and Jan Elway. They were both excited and nervous about their son's game the next day. Following dinner, the four of us were meandering down Bourbon Street, shoulder to shoulder with all of the other frenzied fans who make New Orleans the greatest Super Bowl site in the country. We were able to move one block in about fifteen minutes; the street was packed.

All of a sudden, Jack stopped. He was looking up at a balcony overhanging the street, where television lights were shining on two individuals conducting an interview. One of them was none other than Terry Bradshaw.

Earlier in the week, Bradshaw had uttered some disparaging remarks about John Elway, remarks that Jack took great offense to. Standing there in the middle of the crowd on Bourbon Street, Jack Elway started chanting, "Bradshaw! Bullshit! Bradshaw! Bullshit! Bradshaw! Bullshit!" which people around him started picking up on. The chant became louder and louder, until it was being shouted up and down the entire block and could be heard throughout the French Quarter.

Jack's cheerleading on Bourbon Street didn't bring John or the Broncos any luck the next day as they were thrashed by the Niners, 55-10, but it sure put an end to Bradshaw's interview.

One thing that I have learned over the years working at Easton is to never burn a connection because you never know when it will come back to haunt you or bring you a great experience. The following stories are some examples of how relationships have given me opportunities that I never would have thought would be possible, including chance meetings and once-in-a-lifetime experiences.

••••••••••••••••••••••••

Living Legend

We all have moments in our lives that are unforgettable, and one of those moments for me came when a living legend showed up on the Easton doorstep.

It all started when I received a call from Sandy Sandoval, a representative for Electronic Arts, most widely known as EA Sports. Sandy had formally been a promotion manager at Easton, responsible for the exposure of our slow-pitch softball line. He wanted to order a few baseball bats for a man who starred in some EA Sports video games—a fellow named Muhammad Ali.

Sandy explained that the Champ and his wife, Lonnie, owned a farm in Southern Michigan and planned to build a ball field where all of the kids in the community could come to play. To play ball, they needed bats. I quickly wrote up an order for six bats, and out the door they went.

I totally forgot about it until a month later a letter arrived from Lonnie Ali, thanking me and Easton for our generosity. She stated that the kids enjoyed using the bats and were certainly putting them to good use. It was a nice touch.

About a year later, I was sitting at my desk in Van Nuys when the phone rang. It was Lonnie. She and Muhammad were in Los Angeles for an EA Sports appearance. They wanted to say thanks for the bats and asked if it was fine if they came by the office.

Fine? It was more than fine!

An hour later, a limo pulled up in front of our building, and out stepped the greatest of them all, the man who arguably had the most recognized face in the history of mankind. I simply could not believe it.

I escorted Lonnie and the Champ into our conference room and immediately called my boss, Tony Palma, and Jim Easton. Both dropped what they were doing and joined us. Lunch was ordered in, and an executive assistant was dispatched to a local sporting goods store to purchase as many pairs of boxing gloves and Ali posters she could find. It was also a chance for photographs that couldn't be passed up.

It is well documented that Muhammad Ali suffers from Parkinson's disease. Many of his motor skills have been diminished, including his ability to speak. But Lonnie was able to communicate his messages to us, and the Champ's sense of humor was not lacking in the slightest. For an hour Ali signed autographs and did magic tricks for all of those assembled in our corporate conference room. Then Lonnie turned to me and stated that the Champ wanted to cross the street to our ball bat factory and personally shake hands with each worker, which meant about four hundred handshakes.

It was humorous to observe the reaction of people driving their cars down Haskell Avenue as we waited for them to pass. Brakes screeched and heads turned. I can imagine what they were thinking. *That couldn't be Muhammad Ali?* More telling was the shock on the faces of our people on the factory floor when the Champ just popped up in front of them with his hand out. Jaws dropped that day.

Tony Palma and I throw punches at the Champ in Easton's conference room.

Finally, after three memorable hours, it was time for Muhammad and Lonnie Ali to leave, but not before a moment I will cherish forever. As we were walking back across the street to the corporate office, I asked, "Champ, who gave you the toughest fight?"

He stopped, looked down at me for a few seconds, and then answered in a voice that was crystal clear, sounding just like the old Ali, trading jabs with Howard Cosell. "Joe Frasier," he said, bringing us both back to another time and another era.

With that he ducked into the limo and was gone.

••••••••••••••••••••••••

Surprise meeting at an Easton Party

In the 70s and 80s, Jim Easton was one of the most eligible bachelors in Southern California. He was young (well, maybe middle-aged), athletic, good looking, well-connected, and successful. While any man who watched the TV series *Gilligan's Island* pondered the question "Ginger or Mary Ann?" Jim Easton was one of the few who could potentially give some valuable insight into this dilemma, as it was rumored that he actually dated actress Tina Louise, the striking brunette who played Ginger.

This realm of bachelorhood came to a sudden halt in 1988 when Jim's executive assistant, Toni Mench, introduced him to a strikingly beautiful lady named Phyllis Ludwig. There was definitely a spark between them, but a geographical problem existed. Specifically, as noted, Jim Easton resided in Los Angeles while Ms. Ludwig called Omaha home. As she later told me, "Jim would not travel unless it was business oriented." To Easton's way of thinking, he needed a reason to go to Omaha.

He came up with one. The first game of the College World Series started at 4:00 on Friday afternoon. At the conclusion of that contest, the field was cleared and the maintenance crews took over, readying the diamond for game two. Once the field was dragged, watered, and lined, the next two teams began their warm-up regimens. This whole process took about 90 minutes, and for the fans, dignitaries, and teams not playing there was nothing to do. Rosenblatt Stadium was three miles from downtown Omaha, so there were not too many entertainment options in terms of restaurants and watering holes to kill the time.

Across the street from the stadium, though, was the world-famous Henry Doorly Zoo. Jim Easton came up with a plan to host a reception between games one and two in a private hall at the Zoo's entrance. To stage the event he hired a public relations firm owned by—you guessed it—Phyllis Ludwig.

The "Easton Party," as it became known, turned out to be the biggest social event at the College World Series from its inception in 1989 until 2006, when Jim Easton sold the company. The top names in amateur baseball annually attended, as did countless celebrities and politicians. It was never unusual to be standing in line for food or drink next to the governor of Nebraska, a U.S. senator, or the mayor of Omaha. It was the place to be seen.

A memorable recollection occurred in 2005 when the great Hall of Fame pitcher Bob Gibson (an Omaha native) was holding court at the Easton party. He was chowing down on ribs surrounded by the entire Missouri State baseball team. As one would expect, the kids were in awe, as they should have been. After all, Gibson is arguably one of the greatest pitchers in the history of Major League Baseball.

As I watched the players pound Gibson with question after question, I couldn't help but chuckle. Standing a few feet away from them, engaged in a quiet conversation with Jim Easton, was another world-famous personality: financier Warren Buffet. Mr. Buffet had known Phyllis Ludwig for many years and had come to the Easton receptions as her guest. Always nondescript, as was his reputation, you would never know that he was one of the most influential and wealthiest men in America. I have often wondered how many of those players would like to have that opportunity again to turn their questions elsewhere.

Jim Easton's efforts were worth his while; Phyllis Ludwig became Mrs. Jim Easton in 1994.

•••••••••••••••••••••••••

The President

At times the most important sports stories are not about the games or the star athletes. There are those occasions when the human drama can be far more meaningful, and such was the case for the Keener family.

Steve Keener succeeded Dr. Creighton Hale as President and CEO of Little League Baseball in 1998. Under his leadership and direction, Little League has had significant growth. Every game of their World Series, held in Williamsport, Pennsylvania, is now televised worldwide to huge audiences.

Steve and his wife Cheryl have two sons, Josh and Nick, and wanted to adopt a baby girl. Like many couples in the same situation, they were put on a waiting list, and, as it is in most cases, they were told it could be a long wait.

Finally, they received a call. A baby girl had just been born in a small village in Guatemala, and if they came quickly, they could adopt her. Within days, Steve and Cheryl were headed south.

A week later, Maggie Keener joined her two new brothers at the family home in Williamsport.

Approximately a year and a half later, Steve Keener received a call from a spokesperson for President George W. Bush. Keener was told that the President and Mrs. Bush wanted to attend a game at the Little League World Series, and the they were hoping Steve and Cheryl would sit with them. Keener responded that he would be honored to sit with the

President and First Lady, but that Cheryl would probably not be able to join them, as she would feel uncomfortable leaving eighteen-month-old Maggie with a babysitter. "No problem," the White House spokesperson said. "The President loves children, so you should bring Maggie with you." That sealed the deal.

The President and Mrs. Bush came to Williamsport and joined the Keeners, with Maggie, for a World Series contest. For much of the game, televised across the world, little Maggie Keener, eighteen months removed from living in a thatch hut with a dirt floor and no electricity, plumbing, or running water, was sitting on the lap of the President of the United States of America.

Maybe it is a small world after all.

Every American dreams of having the opportunity to go to the White House and personally meet the President. My chance came in June 2006 when Steve Keener invited me and my wife, Sarah, to be his guests at the "Tee-Ball at the White House" event. Initiated by Steve and President George W. Bush, this was a biannual event where young children of service men and women from around the country were chosen to come play a one-inning game on the South Lawn. The President and First Lady always attended, greeting the kids and giving them a pep talk. Watching five-year-old kids playing ball in front of the President was an incredible sight and, for a few minutes, made the problems of the world seem to disappear. To add to the magic, the game was televised to the military bases overseas so the proud dads and moms serving our country could see their youngsters playing ball and hanging out with the President. It was a cute yet extremely emotional experience.

Little Leaguers getting high-fives on the South Lawn. President Bush is in the background.

The evening before the game, a select group from the Little League party was given a special tour of the West Wing, an area that is usually off-limits to the general public. We were able to view the press briefing room and stand at the podium where the daily briefings are held. Our guide explained to us that the press room is now directly above where the White House swimming pool was once placed—the same pool that Marilyn Monroe was rumored to consort in with President John Kennedy. We also visited the Situation Room, where the President meets regularly with his cabinet and advisors. The highlight was standing and peering into the Oval Office. It almost takes your breath away when you think of the decisions that are made in that room that affect the nation and the world.

A humorous moment occurred when, as we were standing in front of the Oval Office, our young guide made the comment that, due to that late hour, no one of importance was around. Just then, Carl Rove, the controversial aide and advisor to the President, popped his around the corner and stated, "What do you mean no one important?" That garnered a few chuckles and a very red-faced guide.

The biggest treat was the game the next day. President Bush was returning from a European Summit and barely had time to land in the Air Force helicopter, run into the living quarters to change, and hustle out to the South Lawn. He came out in an open shirt and no tie and looked like he was having fun. When the short contest concluded, the President and First Lady shook hands and chatted briefly with each one of us. It was an unforgettable experience.

With President George W. Bush and my wife Sarah at the Little League "Tee-Ball on the South Lawn" in June 2006.

Unfortunately, President Obama did not continue this tradition set by his predecessor. I think it's a shame the tradition stopped because each game on the South Lawn not only helped promote America's pastime, but also created a positive, lifelong experience to many people, young and old alike. It certainly brought a great sense of pride and enjoyment to some of our troops who were stationed away from their families.

••••••••••••••••••••••••
Capitol Hill

Through the efforts of the Sporting Goods Manufacturers Association (SGMA), which in 2013 changed their name to the Sports and Fitness Industry Association (SFIA), I have also been able to spend time on Capitol Hill, meeting with various members of Congress to try to solicit funding for physical education programs at school districts across the United States. It is deplorable that childhood obesity has become one of the largest medical problems our nation faces, yet physical education programs are continually the first cut when school districts attempt to lower their budgets. It is proven that overweight children have a much greater chance of garnering health problems later in life, which adds to our nation's medical budget woes. If there is ever a case for the phrase "penny wise, pound foolish," it is right here in front of us. The cutting of so many physical education programs is a national shame.

Each spring, I—along with many members of the SGMA—climb the Hill to plead with members of Congress for more funding. Tom Cove, the Executive Director of the SGMA, has been relentless in this effort , proving to be a very capable and effective leader. Since 2002, over $700,000,000 has been set aside by Congress. Alas, it is not enough, and we continue to struggle with childhood obesity.

Traversing the halls of the Congressional office building is, like visiting the White House, a sobering and honorable experience. I can simply feel the power of the place just by being there. Each year top athletes join us to fight for the cause. Names like Herschel Walker, Ozzie Smith, Stan Smith, and Steve Garvey have walked the halls, and I personally have been accompanied by baseball stars Gary Carter, John Tudor, Dave Stewart, John Tudor, Tom Candiotti, Jeff Kent, and hockey stalwart Jeremy Roenick. It's always intriguing to observe members of Congress commingling with the celebrities; they all want their pictures taken with the stars and occasionally even ask for game tips. Every year, the Republicans and Democrats play a baseball game at the National's Stadium as a fund raising event, but don't let the fund-raising status fool you. These politicians take this game seriously.

Republicans practicing before the big game against the Democrats at Nationals Stadium.

Both the teams from across the aisle start practices about six weeks prior to the game, usually at 7:00 a.m. at a high school across the Potomac in Virginia. Joe Baca (California) is the traditional starter on the mound for the Democrats, so he likes to ask the pitchers I bring to his office for tips. I chuckle when I think back on Dave Stewart demonstrating the circle change and Tom Candiotti showing the Congressman how to grip the knuckleball.

Former Major League pitcher Dave Stewart showing Congressman Joe Baca how to do the circle change-up grip during the SGMA's Day on Capitol Hill in 2009. Baca was the unspoken leader for the Democrats in their quest to defeat the GOP on the ball diamond.

Several players in that fund-raising baseball game supported our efforts, including Congressman Baca and Republican John Shimkus (Illinois), a tall right-hander who usually starts on the mound for the GOP.

●●●●●●●●●●●●●●●●●●●●●●●●

Standing on George's Head

Speaking of Washington, I can honestly say that I have had the opportunity to walk on George's head.

In 2005, the American Legion World Series was held in Rapid City, South Dakota. At that time, I was serving on the Legion Baseball Scholarship Committee, which met during the event. In a lull between games, Executive Director Jim Quinlan invited me to come along with him and a few others to Mount Rushmore, 35 miles away. One of those others was Dick Green, former star second baseman for the Oakland A's World Series teams of the 70s. A Rapid City resident, Green was intimately involved with the amateur baseball programs in the area and a noted celebrity. In other words, the man had clout. So when we arrived at the national monument, a guide greeted our party and led us up a trail that was off-limits to the public.

A view from our hike up a trail at Mt. Rushmore.

Up we climbed until we were hiking between George Washington and Thomas Jefferson. The trail continued until we were standing on the head of the father of our country with a spectacular view of the Black Hills in all directions. All the tourists down at the visitors center far below looked like little ants scurrying about. It was magnificent and, at the same time, terrifying because getting too close to the edge would've ended in catastrophe. How noted sculptor Gutzon Borglum was able to create such a massive masterpiece is mind-boggling. Every time I see a photo of Mt. Rushmore, I chuckle, thinking of the day I stood on Ol' George's head.

Looking at Thomas Jefferson's nose and Old Abe from the back of George's head. Roosevelt is hidden behind Jefferson.

On top of George's head with (front, left to right) Bill Haase, Sr., VP of
the Hall of Fame; Joe Rudi, former A's All-Star; Jim Quinlan, Executive
Director of American Legion Baseball. To my left in the back row is
another former A's All-Star, Dick Green.

••••••••••••••••••••••••••

The Carrier

In 1999, a gentleman in Los Angeles named Ronnie
Von Gumple called to inquire if Easton would donate some
hockey sticks to a program he had started for underprivileged
children. It turned out that Ronnie, who was retired, served
as the penalty box timer for Los Angeles Kings hockey games
and also spent much of his time helping troubled kids in the
Glendale/Burbank area. The man had a heart of gold. When
I worked out a special program for him, a solid friendship
was established.

Did I mention he had connections, too? In June 1999,
Ronnie invited me and Ed Roski, the owner of the Kings, to
come down to San Diego for a special trip to fly 300 miles on

a navy plane over the Pacific to land on the USS Carrier John C. Stennis. The navy offered such an opportunity to people in high places, like Roski. Another member of the group who boarded the flight out of Coronado Air Station was Gerhard Casper, then the president of Stanford University. I was in select company, and I'm sure some may have been wondering what I was doing there. Sometimes it helps to have a friend like Ronnie Von Gumple.

The aircraft we flew in was a two-engine propeller plane with zero frills. There were no flight attendants with drink carts, and it was so loud that we had to wear ear phones, which served to deaden the noise and allow the pilot to communicate with us. There was one window on the port side of the plane, which I was lucky enough to be sitting next to.

After flying for what seemed like an eternity over an endless ocean, I glanced out the window and there it was, in breathtaking splendor: the Stennis. From our altitude it looked like a little matchbook model. I thought there was no way we could actually land on it. The pilot's voice came through the headphones, explaining that the plane would descend and fly past the carrier, bank hard to port, and then turn upwind to line up with the ship. He also told us that once the wheels hit the deck there would be a little jolt, as the tail hook caught one of the arresting wires. "No worries," he said, "it's all routine."

When the pilot banked the plane to get into line with the flight deck, it felt like the Big Dipper roller coaster at Santa Cruz Beach. And being stopped by a tail hook is not, I repeat not, just a "little" jolt—it's more like hitting a brick wall at 150 miles per hour. What a ride!

Looking out of the window at the Stennis as we circled to get into the landing pattern. I couldn't believe we were really going to try to land on that—it looked like a little toy in a big bathtub!

After lunch with the captain, we were given a tour of the ship. Seeing the teamwork and coordination of the crew is enough to make any American proud; there were over 5,000 people on the Stennis, yet they seemed to work in perfect harmony. The biggest thrill was observing flight operations. It is hard to describe the sense of power you feel when an A6 Intruder or an F-16 revs engines at full throttle and, with a salute from the pilot, is catapulted off the flight deck, going from standstill to 200 MPH in about three seconds!

When I experienced that same launch firsthand, the pilot calmly described the take-off procedure. The plane taxis to the catapult at the bow of the ship, where it is hooked in; then, when clearance is given, the engines are pushed to full throttle. After the pilot salutes to the launch officer, we take off.

Our plane tail-hooking on the flight deck of the John C. Stennis.

The take-off was, for me, not exactly a calming experience. The plane violently vibrated as we waited for the clearance salute, and when the aircraft went hurling off the flight deck, disengaging from the catapult, there was an instant, probably not more than a half a second, where we dropped in altitude. The drop was short but enough to make my heart briefly stop in terror. I started to breathe again when I realized the plane was actually climbing. Three hours later the thrill concluded when the wheels touched the runway in Coronado. There is no ride at Disneyland or Six Flags that will ever top that adventure.

•••••••••••••••••••••••••

Throwing batting practice

One of the biggest thrills of my career occurred in 1981 when Frank Ciensczyk, the Oakland A's equipment manager, rang me up and asked if I wanted to come over to the

Coliseum and throw batting practice that evening. The guy that normally did it was out of town, and his backup was ill.

There was no way I'd say no to pitching in a major league stadium, off a major league mound, and to major league hitters, all while wearing a major league uniform. So what if the job is to let hitters knock the ball 400 feet? I was pretty good at that in real games.

I spent an hour getting roughed up by the A's hitters, loving every minute of it. I guess the A's were pretty satisfied, too, because a couple weeks later, Ciensczyk called again looking for the old right-hander.

Everything was going great; Rickey Henderson rapped out line drive after line drive, and Dwayne Murphy must have hit three of four balls that easily traveled over 450 feet. I had some good stuff that day.

It was going great, that is, until I threw a pitch that was a tad inside and nicked the shoulder of catcher Mike Heath. A 60-mile-per-hour fastball won't hurt a fly, much less a major league hitter, so Heath simply bent over and tossed the ball back to me. Then, five pitches later I flat-out slipped on the rubber and the ball got away from me, drilling Heath right in the small of the back. Again, he just laughed and threw the ball back.

At that moment, from the direction of the A's dugout, a high, shrill voice yelled, "Get him the f— out of here!"

Billy Martin, sounding like he was intoxicated, screamed again, "Get him the f— out of here!"

I'd like it to be known that I may be the only pitcher pulled from batting practice in the history of Major League Baseball.

Billy Martin's favorite batting practice pitcher... until he saw me plunk Mike Heath.

•••••••••••••••••••••••••

First Pitch at Wrigley Field

On the final day of the 1998 major league season, I was in Chicago for a gathering of the SGMA Baseball/Softball Council. The meeting ended ahead of schedule, and finding there were no earlier flights back to California, I decided to call my friend Jay Blunk, the publicity director for the Cubs. I couldn't think of a better way to spend a nice Sunday afternoon than taking in a game at Wrigley Field.

Arriving at the historic ballpark, Jay and I chatted for a while before he nonchalantly inquired if I would be interested in throwing out the ceremonial first pitch. *Would I?* Wow, who could turn that down?

It turned out that there were three first-pitch hurlers that day because the Cubs had also tabbed a couple of people who had been winners of a promotional contest. I never did ask why Jay included me in the parade—maybe a third contest winner got the jitters. Five minutes before game time, the three of us strutted out to the mound to the applause of about twenty-thousand attending fans. Three Cub catchers lined up at home plate to receive the offerings.

The first to throw was a young girl who could not have been over ten years old. Her pitch landed about twelve feet from home plate, and I heard a few groans from the stands.

The second pitch was tossed by a man, who, if I can be kind, may have been at the last Cub's World Series triumph. There were a lot of miles in that old arm. Again, the pitch hit the dirt, and the crowd groaned.

Then it was my turn. It just so happened that I had been playing men's senior baseball that summer and could still throw with a little giddy-up. Certainly more giddy-up than a ten-year-old girl or ninety-year-old man. The poor, unsuspecting catcher, after observing the first two efforts, was not expecting much of a missile coming at him. He didn't have his mitt up when I hurled my pitch. Before he could react, the ball drilled him right in the chest protector. I got a huge round of applause from the crowd, and the poor receiver caught a ton of grief from both dugouts.

●●●●●●●●●●●●●●●●●●●●●●●●●
Put me in, Coach

My pitching career nearly got extended to include MLB games when I asked Ned Colletti to put me on the roster. I got to know Ned during his tenure as the Assistant GM of the

San Francisco Giants in the early 2000s. Then, in November 2005, he left the Giants to take over the reins as General Manager for the arch-rival Los Angeles Dodgers.

Just for fun, in all of my emails or text messages to Ned I always reminded him that, if the need were to arise, the old right-hander (me) was available and for a very cheap price— he wouldn't even have to negotiate with an agent. I could just picture him rolling his eyes each time I sent this. Usually he simply ignored it, but, occasionally he let me know where I could take my recommendation—all in fun, of course.

In 2009, the Dodgers opened their new spring training facility in Glendale, Arizona, and Ned arranged tickets for me, Sarah, and Bob and Sally Mehaffey, best friends from our college days, to attend a game against the Colorado Rockies. I was excited to see the new yard and starter Chad Billingsley, the highly touted young pitcher.

Alas, things did not really go well for the home team. Billingsley was roughed up, and after a parade of Dodger pitchers, the contest mercifully concluded with the Rockies plating nineteen runs. The game was not good for the Dodgers, but we had a great time. The seats were terrific. So on the drive back to our hotel, I emailed Ned to thank him. His reply was priceless: "That was brutal. One more horseshit pitcher and you were next!"

That's about as close as I got to being in the majors.

* *

The National Anthem

Like any father, I wanted to make the wishes of my children come true. My son, Michael, wanted to work as a bat boy at a Major League game, and I was really pleased when he served in that role for the Pittsburgh Pirates when they played the Giants at Pac Bell Park in 2000.

Like many kids, my daughter, Sally, had a dream to sing the National Anthem before a Giants game when she was thirteen years old. One benefit of being in the sporting goods industry is being acquainted with influential people. For me, one such person was Jorge Costa, senior VP of Stadium Operations for the San Francisco Giants. Over lunch one day, I happened to mention Sally's wish, and Jorge said if she was really serious, she should make a demo tape and forward it to him. He said he'd see what he could do.

Sally spent hours practicing and then cut the demo, which I forwarded to Jorge. Not long afterward, he called and gave a date a week away, prior to an inter-league match up with the Tampa Bay Devil Rays. Sally was really excited and practiced all week; she sounded great with no sign of fear or nervousness. Just confidence.

On the big day, Jorge told me to have Sally at the ballpark at 2:00 p.m. so she could do a dry-run with the full microphone. One thing you learn is that sound travels slowly; when the person sings into the microphone, the sound over the loudspeakers may be delayed for a second, which was why it was important that Sally experience this before the real thing. In addition, I was sure the Giants operations staff wanted to be sure that Sally could really sing.

And sing she did. The mike-check anthem was beautiful with no glitches. The problem then was to kill time. Sally wasn't scheduled to sing the anthem until 7:15 p.m., and the practice run was finished at 3:00. I suggested we take a walk outside the stadium. As we were going out the gate we bumped into former all-star Vida Blue, who was then doing public relations work for the Giants. I introduced Vida to

Sally and informed him that she was going to sing the anthem that night.

"Oh, that's great, honey," Vida said. "You'll do great. One thing, though—don't forget the words."

Forget the words? That wasn't even on Sally's mind, or mine, until he said it. Thanks a lot, Vida! Any more tips?

We went to a local hamburger joint and went over the verses again and again. In my own fear, I had confused poor Sally so much that only the good man upstairs knew what would come out of her voice box when the bell rang. I even wrote down the words on a napkin, just in case. I couldn't get over the fear that I had fostered another Rosie O'Donnell, who had embarrassed herself singing the anthem in front of a huge television audience.

Finally, at 7:15, Sally was introduced by the stadium announcer, and she boldly strode to the microphone in front of the pitchers mound. In front of a shaking father and 37,000 fans, she banged out a beautiful rendition of the Star Spangled Banner.

●●●●●●●●●●●●●●●●●●●●●●●●

Coaching in the NFL

One of the more odd, but true, statements I have ever made is that I served as a coach in the National Football League.

Seriously.

The biggest annual meat market is the National Invitational Camp, initiated in 1982 in Tampa, Florida, by National Football Scouting, Inc. Commonly known as the NFL Scouting Combine, the key purpose then, as it is today, was to ascertain medical information on the top draft eligible prospects in college football. The inaugural NIC was attended by a total of 163 players and established a foundation for future expansion.

During the first three years, two additional camps were held at different times to collect similar information for teams that did not belong to National Football Scouting. One of those camps was held at the Superdome in New Orleans.

As mentioned in an earlier chapter, John Beake, the General Manager of the Denver Broncos, was a huge help to us in our quest to sign John Elway to the shoe endorsement deal with Mizuno. In January 1984, following Elway's rookie season, Beake invited me to come to New Orleans and serve on the coaching staff for the Broncos at the Combine. The Broncos must have been keen to absorb my football knowledge, which was about zero. In reality, my job was to hold a clipboard and write down the pertinent information from the tests the players were being subjected to, such as the 40-yard dash and vertical jump. I'm sure a lot of people were wondering, "Who's the wimpy guy wearing the Broncos coaching staff shirt?"

At the hotel one night, head coach Dan Reeves put on quite a show blowing quarters from under a dining room table into a drinking glass. Had that been one of the players' tests, Reeves could have played a few more years. He was a real pro!

At the conclusion of the Combine, while waiting for my flight out, I noticed another guy also waiting to catch his. Younger than me, he had also been on the Broncos staff. Like me, he really did not seem like a "football guy." I thought maybe he had also been there to hold a clipboard. That proved to be an example of my ability to evaluate football talent, either in players or coaches because, you see, the young coach waiting in the boarding lounge was Mike Shanahan, who later led the Broncos to consecutive Superbowl victories in 1997 and 1998. It's probably a good thing I was never trusted with more than the clipboard, what with my natural eye for scouting football talent.

•••••••••••••••••••••••••

A gripping story

Standing on the sidelines of an NFL game is an eye-opening experience. I know because that's where I was one night in Denver when the Broncos were hosting the 49ers in a Monday night tilt.

I was there at the invitation of Michael Zagaris, the Niners team photographer. It wasn't to simply be a spectator; I was brought along to serve as the gripper—the person who had to carry all of the cameras. NFL photographers use a variety of cameras and lenses to shoot the action, and since they can't snap away and hold bags at the same time, grippers get the job.

While that may sound like fun, I promise you it is serious work. The photographer wants access to every camera and lens the gripper is carrying, and he wants it now! He can't afford to miss an opportune shot, so photographer and gripper are always on the move around the perimeter of the field.

It just so happened that on that particular night a major snowstorm was blowing in from the Rockies. In fact, it was the game that is known in NFL history as the "snowball game." As Ray Wersching, the 49er placekicker, was lining up for a short field goal attempt, a fan from the second deck threw a snowball that landed right in front of the holder, which upset the timing of the play. Wersching missed the kick, and the Broncos triumphed in a very close game.

The snowball play was crazy, but it was the antics of Zagaris and the Broncos fans that made this game memorable for me. In the fourth quarter, with plenty of time for the fans to get liquored up, the taunts directed toward the 49er players was getting downright ugly. Finally, Zagaris could not take it anymore. He turned around and announced to the Denver faithful, with the middle finger of both hands, who he thought was number one.

That was all it took. The next thing I knew, we were ducking every object within throwing distance. I think some of the fans were pretending to be John Elway, but instead of throwing a football, they threw whiskey bottles, beer bottles, hot dogs, ice, snowballs, and pretty much anything they could get their hands on. All these things were flying through the air, directed toward Zagaris, and there I was right next to him.

I wasn't there for long, though. I dropped the camera bags like they were hot potatoes and was out of there in a flash, but not before being covered with mustard and catsup and smelling like a brewery.

That ended my career as a gripper in a snapshot.

Mike Zagaris snapped this shot moments before he showed the Bronco fans who he thought was number one. The Niners player is cornerback Eric Wright.

●●●●●●●●●●●●●●●●●●●●●●●●●

Fantasy Camp

One of the more clever ideas that has sprung up in the past thirty years is the "fantasy camp" that is put on by most Major League ball clubs. For a fairly large fee (usually around $4,000), an adult can sign up to go to a team spring training facility for a week of hanging out with retired former players and playing ball.

In April 1990, my boss, Doug Kelly, came to me with a plan. Easton would pay for me to go to the Giants fantasy camp with the goal that I was to write an article about the experience and get it published in various media outlets.

Former San Francisco players Jim Barr and Chris Speier check out the campers during batting practice before a game.

So off to Arizona I went, and following is my story that ran in the *San Francisco Examiner* on July 14, 1990.

Say hey, it was a Giant thrill
Local fan has his fantasies fulfilled at over-30 camp

Editor's note: Jim Darby, the west coast representative for Easton baseball equipment, is a regular at the Oakland Coliseum and Candlestick Park. He recently spent a week at the Giants' fantasy camp and filed this report.

By Jim Darby
Special to the Examiner

Tempe, Ariz.— I've heard umpires yell "Play ball" a million times in my life. This time it was different. I was the one playing ball with the major-leaguers.

"Now batting for the Giants, No. 24, Willie Mays," the announcer's voice carried across the outfield. The pitcher winds up as I position myself at shortstop. Mays hits a hard shot to my left. I reach for the ball, and…

Was this a fantasy? A little fantasy and reality came together in the Arizona desert. It was the Giants' fantasy camp. The camp is open to anyone over 30 and provides the chance to experience life as a major-leaguer. For one week the campers play in major-league spring training parks, dress in major-league uniforms, receive treatment on sore muscles from major league trainers and are managed by the players we watched in our childhood.

All the fantasy campers arrived at Phoenix Sky Harbor Airport on a Sunday afternoon. After a short bus ride to the Westcourt in the Buttes resort, the first official team meeting took place. Seventy-seven campers introduced themselves, along with their reason for living the fantasy.

Explanations varied, with the obvious being: "I've always wanted to see what it's like to be a major leaguer." The star of the day went to the guy who said, "I've wanted to come to this for three years, but my wife wouldn't let me. Well, I was divorced 10 days ago, and …."

The campers were made up from men from all walks of life. There were doctors, attorneys, retailers, artists, teachers, publishers, entertainers, firemen, salesmen, CPA's, computer technicians and authors. The one common denominator was that they all wanted to lead the life of a major-leaguer, if only for a week.

Monday—Draft day

In the morning, the 77 hopefuls were fully decked out in Giants uniforms for stretching exercises under the watchful eye of a professional training staff.

Drills at outfield, infield, catching, pitching and hitting stations followed under the scrutiny of the skippers, whose names reflect the glory days of the '60s and '70s: Orlando Cepeda, Tom Haller, Mike McCormick, Ed Bailey, Jim Barr, Hobie Landrith, Jim Ray Hart, John "The Count" Montefusco, Chris Speier, Mike Sadek and

John D'Aquisto. That evening, the pros presided over the draft, and participants were selected for six teams.

Tuesday—Opening day

Reporting to the locker room, I found that I was selected by Gar's Gators, managed by Ed Bailey. Bailey and Haller caught for the Giants in the 1962 World Series. Ed Bailey—it seems like yesterday that I heard Giants announcer Russ Hodges screaming into the radio about Bailey charging the mound after a brushback from Pirates fastballer Bob Friend. Bailey then knocked Friend's next pitch out of Forbes Field in Pittsburgh. Now Forbes Field is gone, replaced by modern Three Rivers Stadium, and Bailey is sharing a few memories and creating a few others.

Before the first game, we were all introduced to Kangaroo Court, which would become a morning ritual. Presided over by Judge Mike "Shiek" Sadek, no one, not even the coaches, was exempt from this bizarre form of justice. Accusations and quick convictions were rampant. We were stung for such crimes as pitching while wearing sunglasses, taking a woman (usually wives) into the dugout, tripping while rounding bases and sundry other offenses.

One player, late in the week, was fined just because he hadn't been fined yet. No one was safe. And no one complained. The $1 fines went to tip the clubhouse men who cleaned and prepared the uniforms each day.

We played two games on Tuesday, against Hobie Landrith's Players and the Morgana Mikes, managed by Mike McCormick. Each game went six innings and everyone played. The games were competitive but not at the expense of losing their fun. Every hit, throw, error, strikeout, walk, slide and diving play brought back memories. There is no feeling that compares to returning to the fields of our youth.

By the way, Gar's Gators swept 'em.

Wednesday—Getting serious

After Kangaroo Court, the competition became a little more serious. The A's were coming to play. Sportsworld, which sponsors the event, also hosts an Oakland A's fantasy camp in the Phoenix area. Today we played a home-and-away double-header—a morning game at our park, then an afternoon contest in Phoenix.

Giants and A's fantasy campers played eight games. And for die-hard Giants fans, the World Series sweep of '89 has been avenged.

The Giants' campers took seven of the eight—two wins for Gar's Gators.

Thursday—A sweep

Gar's Gators did it again—a sweep of Cepeda's Bulls and Haller's Hackers.

By this time we had all discovered the most important room in the stadium—the training room. With the average age of the campers being 39, the trainers earned their keep. Ice packs, aspirin, Ace bandages, and rubdowns were an everyday necessity. Surprisingly the injuries were kept to a minimum. There were a few pulled and aching muscles, but that was to be expected. The most serious injury was the guy who tripped over his spikes in the bathroom and cut his hand on the towel dispenser. He required a few stitches. I can just see him explaining that one to the boys back home.

Friday—The media

Steve Bitker, a reporter for radio station KNBR in The City, the Giants' flagship, interviewed many of the campers on how it felt beating the A's campers. We were still talking to the press.

Bitker is a camper himself, playing for Haller's Hackers. When asked what his most interesting experience at the camp had been, he said, "Playing catcher for the first time ever (at the age of 36)."

Gar's Gators swamped Montefusco's Count's Colts in the morning game to finish the regular season at 7-0 (counting two wins over the A's).

The culmination of this fantasy came on Friday night and Saturday afternoon when each team played a scrimmage game against the camp coaches and managers at Tempe Diablo Stadium.

Our club was introduced along the first-base foul line, but the fans—there really were a few—were not there to root for Gar's Gators. Their cheers were directed toward the players lining up on the third-base foul line. It dawned on me just where we were when I heard the names being announced, a roll call of Giants greats that concluded with the greatest Giant—Willie Mays.

Each camper played against the former stars for three innings. We held the Giants scoreless but, unfortunately, Mike McCormick and John D'Aquisto shut us down, too. No matter. I came home with a million memories. Most particularly the play where this all started—the ball ripped by Willie snapped into my glove on the second hop. I quickly spun around and gunned (others might say tossed) to the stretching first baseman. The ball and Mays arrived together in a flash of a second, but my throw nipped the Greatest by a millisecond. The umpire's fist went into the air, and I realized that I had thrown out a legend, my boyhood idol.

And that was no fantasy.

What could make any player feel like a Big Leaguer? His own baseball card, of course. All the campers were given their own stack of cards, which, unfortunately, were not worth much on the collectibles market.

EPILOGUE

Extra Innings

To use a phrase from *Butch Cassidy and the Sundance Kid*, "You get older every day. Now that's a law…"

Change comes as time rolls along. In March 2006, Jim Easton sold the company to a private equity firm that already owned Riddell, Giro, and Bell Helmets. From that point forward, we became known as Easton-Bell Sports. Consolidating companies also changed the organization structure. Most of the upper management from Easton Sports has been replaced (some on their own volition, some not) by a younger group of people, which, of course, has brought a new marketing mentality. Social networking has taken over with terms like Facebook, tweeting, and blogs as the basis of how companies reach out to young consumers today. We still try to work with top athletes but certainly look to align with those who understand the value of the new medium and are willing to work with us along those lines.

Over time my interaction with professional baseball players became less and less, and I spent more time on legislative affairs. Many of my friends and associates asked if I missed working with the athletes, and my answer was a definitive "No!"

That may sound crazy to some, but, with any endeavor, things change over time. When I started with the Curley-Bates Company in 1977, the sporting goods reps worked directly with the players, and friendships were established out of those initial contacts. Today, almost all the interaction with the players is through their agents.

The first player I signed to an endorsement deal was Dusty Baker of the Dodgers, four months after he had been named MVP of the National League Championship Series. We basically agreed to the terms of the deal while driving together between Santa Maria, California, and Los Angeles. No agent participated or was even needed. The agreed upon fee was $1,500 guaranteed, along with a small royalty on gloves sold if we decided to imprint his name (which we did). That may not seem like much, but in those days Dusty wasn't making much more than $100,000 from the Dodgers. Obviously, things have changed since 1977. With the average salary for major league ballplayers today landing well into the millions, the amounts that sporting goods companies can offer the everyday player may seem like a trifle. The players, and their agents, expect more and usually get it. It used to get under the skins of the agents when I inquired what their take was in the fee the player received, as I knew it could get as high as twenty percent. I told them we had a deal if they took off the twenty percent. Of course, they always refused. Their twenty-percent cut is why agents always want to deal in cash rather than talking compensation via product-in-kind: It's hard to take twenty percent of a set of golf clubs, an automobile, or a stereo system.

Today, it isn't unusual to see mid-level players making thousands of dollars on endorsement deals, particularly if they are in the right ball club. Players on high media teams like the Yankees, Red Sox, Cubs, Angels, or Dodgers make off like bandits. Many times we would negotiate a lower fee, or an out option, if the player we had on one of those clubs was traded to a team that received less media exposure.

It is tough to get close even to minor league players today. They also tend to have agents, which means they want something other than just free gloves, shoes, and batters gloves. In the 1970s and 1980s, I used to go to the Arizona and Florida Instructional camps that the major league clubs held for their top prospects. I laid out the ball gloves and cleats for the players to see and try on, hoping to ink them on the spot. The normal deal was a ten-year commitment for two gloves and two pairs of cleats per year. Of course, the player was obligating himself to exclusively use the company's products. This may not seem like much today, but the players loved it, and many jumped at the opportunity. I was able to sign many young, future stars to these agreements, such as Don Mattingly, Dave Stewart, and Dave Dravecky. Usually, if the player went on to the major leagues and became a star, we would, without an agent, work out a new agreement that reflected the player's new status.

Pro hockey players are a bit different than their baseball cousins. Most rely on obtaining the product that best suits their game. Many of the biggest stars in the NHL, such as Joe Sakic, Brett Hull, Peter Forsberg, and Paul Kariya, used Easton sticks because they believed they were the best for their game. Money was not the motivating factor—performance was. As Kariya once told me, "I can make a lot more money being a better hockey player than I can endorsing your sticks." Sound wisdom.

Joe Sakic on October 1, 2009, the night the Colorado Avalanche retired his number. Also in the picture are, from left to right, Global Marketing Manager Mark Hughes, pro rep Boyd Sutton, manager of pro stick manufacturing Mike McGrath, me, and Joe's son, Mitch. Sakic was terrific to work with. The only thing he demanded was that his Easton sticks be made to his specifications and that they be delivered on time.

The NCAA has not stayed put over the past few years, either. In the 2011 season, a new standard for non-wood bats was inaugurated: the Baseball Bat Coefficient of Restitution, or BBCOR. It would take a physicist to understand the science of what all this means. To compare the difference between the new BBCOR standard versus the old BESR, I will state it very simply (as I see it): BESR made non-wood bats "similar to wood," while BBCOR bats are designed to hit "like wood." It has yet to be determined if this will be good for the amateur game going forward. The baseball purists may think the new standard is terrific; however, at the 2011 College World Series in Omaha, the teams combined for a total of only nine homeruns, the lowest total in over 40 years.

In the "instant gratification" world that we live in today, such a drop-off in offensive production may not be in the long-term best interest of the sport. As the Nike ad in the late 1990s so eloquently pointed out, "Chicks dig the long ball…" So, we'll see. Only time will tell how those changes will affect the sport.

At times Major League Baseball could make life difficult for manufacturers. One particular instance stands out in my mind. In April 1981, three years after we had introduced the Mizuno line of ball gloves to the players, I received a letter from the Commissioner's office stating that our gloves could no longer be used because the "M" logo was too shiny. At first I thought it was a joke but realized it was serious when I started receiving calls from players who told me that umpires had told them they couldn't play with their Mizuno gloves. A disaster was brewing. The season had already started, so there was no way we could make new custom gloves with new logos overnight. The solution, though, was right around the corner at our local hardware store. I purchased hundreds of sheets of sandpaper, slapped a small Mizuno logo on each piece, and sent them overnight to hundreds of major and minor league players across the country. I also enclosed a form letter to each player, requesting that he use the "official" Mizuno sandpaper to rub off the shine on the logo. The ploy worked perfectly. Umpires could not throw out the gloves if the logo wasn't shiny. We even picked up some favorable press, as the scribes realized what a farce the whole situation was.

Over time, the media has changed, too, and it has been a rare time that the press has been kind to us. With the coming of the internet, accuracy in reporting has taken second place to who can break the story first, whether correct or not.

Sensation has become the buzz word, not the truth. Many times I was interviewed by journalists writing about the wood versus non-wood bat issue only to have my quotes chopped out because the facts I gave ruined the sensationalist story they were seeking—or, worse, I was misquoted. Requests for rebuttals normally were ignored or appeared in an obscure section of the newspaper.

In the late 90s, when the debate regarding the performance of non-wood bats was at its peak, I was interviewed by a writer from the *Wall Street Journal*. He wanted to know why the NCAA and manufacturers were butting heads over the standards that the NCAA Rules Committee was planning to implement. I gave him all of the information that I had accumulated in terms of safety data, offensive statistics, and the increasing growth and popularity of the college game. The interview took over an hour, and he certainly seemed to grasp everything I was telling him. Heck, he was even agreeing with me.

As the interview concluded, I was asked, "Off the record, what do you think is motivating the Rules Committee to look into making changes in the performance of the bats?" Since he had specified this was off the record, I jokingly replied, "Heck, they're just a bunch of yahoos with nothing better to do." He laughed, thanked me for the interview, and hung up.

Of course, I was really excited. This was the *Wall Street Journal*, not some small town periodical. I was going to be featured and could not wait for all of my buddies and work associates to see my name in lights. When the article came out, I rushed out and bought ten copies. Returning to my office, I tore through the paper, looking for my quotes and all of the information that I had offered up. The only quotes I saw, however, were from members of the Rules Committee,

stating that the bats had to be toned down because they felt
the game was out of balance. At the end of the article, I found
my name, stating that I thought the NCAA Baseball Rules
Committee was made up of a bunch of yahoos. So much for
"off the record."

With time, most of the top athletes who initially helped
build the Easton and Mizuno brands retired as players,
though some have stayed involved in the game. Dusty Baker
and Bobby Valentine, the first two players I ever signed to
endorsement contracts, have managed multiple teams in the
big leagues. Bob Boone is the Assistant GM and Director of
Player Development for the Washington Nationals (he has
also watched two of his sons in major league careers of their
own). Steve Yzerman is the General Manager of the Tampa
Bay Lightning, while John Elway has gone on to the position
of Vice-President of Football Operations for his beloved
Broncos.

The Halls of Fame have been active, as well. Many former
players who had ties to Easton Sports or the early days of
Mizuno have received the call for their sport. Entering
Cooperstown have been names like Goose Gossage, Ozzie
Smith, Rickey Henderson, Gary Carter, and Robin Yount.
The Pro Football HOF in Canton, Ohio, has added the names
of Charlie Joiner, Randy White, Steve Young, John Elway,
and Joe Montana. And in Toronto, the Hockey Hall of Fame
has inducted Easton players Wayne Gretzky, Brian Leetch,
Steve Yzerman, Brett Hull, Mark Howe, Peter Forsberg, Mike
Modano, Brendan Shanahan, and Joe Sakic. More names
should be called in the next few years, most notably, Paul
Kariya, Jeremy Roenick, and Nick Lidstrom. Jeff Kent is
certainly due a call from Cooperstown. After all, he was the
most prolific hitting second baseman in the history of Major

290

Right Off the Bat

League Baseball.

One name conspicuously absent from HOF notoriety is Pete Rose. How can the all-time hit king not be in the Hall of Fame? He certainly didn't rap out 4,256 hits by wagering with the hundreds of pitchers he faced. In 2009, I attended Rickey Henderson's induction ceremony, along with my old compatriots George Sheldon and Doug Kelly. As we toured the museum in Cooperstown, I noticed that a showcase was set up for each team in the major leagues with products on display that had been used by key players on the ball club. In the showcase for the Cincinnati Reds, there were a number of items that had been used by Pete Rose. I think it's a downfall for the HOF that they pretend he never existed while including the products he used to be put on display.

Thirty years following my entrée into the sporting goods business, I had the honor to attend, as a guest of Major League Baseball, the All-Star game at Yankee Stadium, which was the last to be played at the "House That Ruth Built." It was my first venture to the famed ball park in the Bronx, and as I sat watching all the stars being introduced, both past and present, it was easy to fantasize about all the events that had taken place there, including the Babe swatting out his 60th homerun in 1927, followed by Roger Maris knocking out number 61 thirty-four years later. What fan could visit Yankee Stadium and not visualize the grace of Joe DiMaggio, the power of Mickey Mantle, or Yogi Berra jumping into the arms of Don Larsen following Larsen's perfect game in the 1956 World Series?

Reflecting back on these historic sports events made me realize that the past thirty years had been a fantasy come true for me. In December 1977, I would have considered someone drunk, stoned, or crazy if they had suggested that

I would have a career that allowed me to work with some of the great sports figures of our era, including names like Elway, Montana, Gossage, Rose, Gretzky, Yzerman, and the greatest of them all, Muhammad Ali. Yet, in its quirky way, fate led me down that road, and what a great ride—not to mention a great learning experience—it has been. If there is one lesson I can take from my on-the-job education, it is that relationships mean everything. In the sporting goods business world, relationships = championships.

Like athletes, people who work in the promotion of sporting goods equipment have their own battles to fight. Sometimes they win; sometimes they don't. The next time you see a copy of *Sports Illustrated*, take a closer look at the products on the cover. Somewhere there is a promo guy or gal jumping for joy over their huge victory.

About the Author

Photo taken by Shelley Castellano.

A 37-year veteran of the sporting goods industry, Jim Darby has worked with hundreds of top athletes, including over 20 Hall-of Famers from the National Hockey League, National Football League, and Major League Baseball. Named the University of California, Berkeley baseball alumnus of the year in 2008, he has also been inducted into the Halls of Fame for the United States Sports Specialties Association (USSSA), Men's Senior Baseball, and the National High School Baseball Coaches Association (NHSBCA).